glow
a conversation in reflecting
the Light of the World

randy ross

FIRST SILVER THREAD PUBLISHING EDITION, OCTOBER 2010
All rights reserved. No part of this book may be reproduced, scanned, or distributed in any printed or electronic form without written permission. Please do not participate in or encourage piracy of copyrighted materials in violation of the author's rights.

Silver Thread Publishing is a division of A Silver Thread, LLC. Colorado 2009
www.asilverthread.com

Cover design and photograph by Austyn Elizabeth Photography, LLC
www.austynelizabeth.com

Publisher has no control over or does not assume any responsibility for Author or third-party websites or their content.
Copyright 2010 by Silver Thread Publishing
Cover photograph Copyright 2010 by Austyn Elizabeth Ford
Illustrations Copyright 2010 by A Silver Thread, LLC
Font Copyright Fonthead Design Inc.
ISBN 978-0-9844129-7-6
Printed in the United States of America

This book is dedicated to my dad, Harvey Ross. You and mom taught me to glow Jesus in any and all of life's situations. Even though you have been gone for nearly a dozen years, your memory still manages to reflect the Light of the World. I sure do miss you…

chapter summaries

introduction   pg 1
The Great Commission is given to all followers of Jesus, not as a neat idea, but rather as an expectation. So, if all of us are supposed to share our faith, why do we find evangelism so difficult? What exactly is Jesus asking of us?

chapter one   pg 17
a burning within, glowing out
If all followers of Christ were reflecting Jesus to the world around them, what would that look like? Using characteristics of a disco ball and a little trip to Emmaus, evangelism is presented as a natural and organic response to the Light of the World taking up residence in His followers.

chapter two   pg 43
what keeps us from shining bright?
The ideal presented in Chapter 1 is a rarity in our world … even though we all have the same light. So why aren't we reflecting Christ effectively? Uncover a number of "dimmer switches" that restrict the natural glow that we, as followers of Christ, could and should have.

chapter three — pg 71
we glow brighter when we spend time in the Son

Using the biblical example of Moses, you'll be challenged to have regular interaction with your maker as a means of increasing your glowing effectiveness in sharing your faith. Find out what a glow-in-the-dark Frisbee has to do with reflecting the Light of the World. Spiritual applications like vision, instruction, construction, passion, and zeal are identified as core desires of time spent alone with God.

chapter four — pg 95
we glow brighter when we are under pressure

Just as the childhood Glow-Worm was ineffective until squeezed, we are given occasion to glow Jesus when those around us see us under pressure. The apostle Paul was great at this. Learn the importance of persevering, checking your attitude, and finishing strong, because when the going gets tough, the world takes notice of those who claim to have an answer.

chapter five — pg 111
we glow brighter when we are broken

The moments of life when we are humbled and broken can provide us with great opportunities to allow Christ to be seen in and through us. Looking at the Scriptural account of Mary anointing Jesus' feet with oil and the image of a glowstick, find encouragement to reveal the foundational building blocks of humility and brokenness in your journey as you glow Jesus to your friends and family.

chapter six   pg 139
we glow brighter when we display our powerlessness

Sometimes Jesus is more clearly seen, not as we enter into situations, not with answers, fix-it manuals or recovery plans, but as we simply share the pain and tears of others. A look at the time Jesus' friend Lazarus died and the way Job's friends responded to his pain illustrate that having the right thing to say isn't always as important as just being there. The security of ornamental lawn lamps serve as an illustration to the comfort that just a little glowing light can provide to situations where words won't take the problems away.

conclusion   pg 163

So what's next? Where do you start to glow? The sky's the limit, though some want to put ceilings on evangelism that restrict it to certain techniques and locations. But we are to "glow" into all the world, not just the pretty parts of it.

resources

Visit www.randy-ross.com/downloads for free resources.
- *GLOW group discussion questions for your book club.*
- *GLOW teacher's guide*
- *GLOW hand-outs for your small group*

Illustration Nº· 1 The Banana

introduction

My friend Rob told me about this guy in his church who said that he wanted God to give him the opportunity to talk about Jesus with someone during the next 24 hours. So he's driving his car down the road and this guy flags him down. He pulls up to the guy to see what he needs. The stranger says, "Just take me to the 7-Eleven." So the stranger hops in the guy's car and they are off, driving nowhere near any known convenience stores, not to mention a 7-Eleven.

"Is there even a 7-Eleven around here?" he asks. The guy reaches over, throws the car in park and takes the driver's keys. "Just give me all your money," the stranger demands, thrusting a concealed gun in his coat at the driver/victim. "Here's 13 bucks … it's all I have," Rob's friend says. "But what you really need is not my money. Do you know Jesus? 'Cause you really need to get your butt in a church sometime!"

"Oh, man!!" the robber exclaims. He was understandably frustrated. Not only is he only getting a measly 13 bucks out of this heist, but now he's set up for a lecture from a Jesus freak! So, he tries to get out of the car, but the passenger door doesn't work. "I knew God was gonna' do this to me if I tried to pull a stunt like this!" A few minutes later, the gunman is talking about how he used to go to church, and how he quit going because it got boring or there were too many hypocrites or whatever. The driver invites the stranger to go to church with him, and the gunman says it's not a bad idea. He asks where the driver goes to church. The driver whips out his Bible, grabs a piece of paper, and writes down info about the church. Then the gunman grabs the Bible, whips out a knife, etches his phone number on the cover of it, and says, "Call me. I want to go to church with you sometime."

The gunman confesses he doesn't even have a gun. It was a banana or something. He tries to give the 13 bucks back, but is denied. "Consider it a loan," says the driver. "You can just pay me back some Sunday at church." Sometimes God answers prayer in the weirdest ways.

Then it hits me: I am so like this guy from my friend Rob's church. And I know I am not alone. I usually need to be at gunpoint to even want to share my faith. I know it's the Great Commission and all. I know Rick Warren says it is one of the purposes for which I was created. But I hate to witness. Visions of street evangelists and door-to-door proselytizers invade my mind, and I cringe. I shrink back from the responsibility my Savior has entrusted me with.

I once told a friend that if there was a show called The Fear Factor for Jesus Followers, the final round of feats would go like this: "Okay, you've eaten locusts and wild honey; you've survived the recreated plagues of Egypt; and even managed to wallow in whale guts just like Jonah. Now, for the big money, your last feat is to … tell someone about Jesus." No way. All of the money I could win, all of the stuff I could buy, all of the places I could visit, all of the charities I could support … No way. I just don't think I could. I'd lose.

Why are people so afraid to talk to people about Jesus? Why am I so afraid? I mean, I've done it. I've been a part of leading numerous people into a relationship with Jesus. But it still kind of freaks me out. I'm reluctant—hesitant, almost. Timid would be a good word too. What is it that makes this so frightening to so many Jesus Followers? We need courage, and sometimes there is a shortage of that particular ingredient. But maybe we need to understand what courage really is. Courage is not living without fear; rather, it is the determination to be led by something greater.

What causes people to hesitate in talking about Jesus with people?

{ Throughout this book you'll find a number of questions followed by gray boxes. The boxes provide an opportunity for you to join the conversation. Write in your thoughts and discuss them with your friends. }

i don't know what to say

One reason people hesitate in talking about Jesus is the fear that we won't know what to say. When I was in eighth grade, there was this girl I had a crush on. She was a beautiful, petite, blonde girl. I so wanted to ask her to go with me. (Just where a 13-year-old is supposed to go, I still don't know.) It was serious. I thought about her all the time. I dreamed of the happiness I knew I'd have just holding her hand on the way home from school, even though I didn't know where she lived. And now I can't even remember her name! It's funny how things change. We'd talk a lot, me, her friends, and my friends, and I just wanted to blurt out, "Hey blonde girl (whose name I can't remember), I so want to be your boyfriend! How about it?"

Okay, so the words would've been much smoother than that back then, but you get the picture. So this one day I gathered all of the strength in my measly 90-pound body and called her house. This was it! I was gonna' tell her. 266- ... I called the number, she answered, and ... Yep, total silence. I had no idea what to say. I'd planned out my words and selected just the right ones to speak of my love and admiration. And when the time came, when the pressure was on, when the rubber met the road, I choked. Then I hung up the phone and never called her again. I never did tell her my feelings, so she never entered into a relationship with me.

Many people have the same problem with sharing their faith. They think about what they'd say to their friend. It's rehearsed and even written out. The desire is there. Unfortunately, the words aren't. They choke. The opportunity passes, paralyzed by the almighty what-if. What if they ask me questions I can't answer? What if I screw the whole thing up? What if I _____ (insert your worst fear of speaking here).

Read Luke 12:11-12 and 21:13-15. What do these verses have to do with not knowing what to say when you talk to people about Jesus?

i don't want to be insensitive

Another thing that keeps people from sharing their faith is that they don't want to shove religion at people in fear of offending others. Neither do I, and Jesus doesn't want us to do this either. I think He hates religion with all that is in Him. I've had strangers at the airport stop and try to convert me while I'm trying to connect with my next flight. I've had strangers interrupt my dinner in order to try their hand at converting me to their path of enlightenment, offering me their infomercials, magazines, and phone calls. I wouldn't employ the same techniques because I don't want religion shoved at me either! I met this lady who feels like God wants her to go around to various neighborhoods one day a week, knock on the doors of strangers, and ask them, "If you died today, do you know for sure you wouldn't go to hell?" It's pretty much like drive-by proselytizing. I'm surprised she doesn't get punched in the face at least once a week. I mean, I'd hit her!

The thing is that she's really not offering anything. The Message of Jesus is one of hope. Sure, there is responsibility and conviction and judgment, but ultimately, Jesus' Message is one of faith and hope, grace, and mercy, not rules, threats, and fear. I find the Message of Jesus to be very different than the message of many of those who practice the religion bearing His name. Relationship is what Jesus offers and what He asks me to offer for Him. Religion is very different. I find religion offensive even if it's not shoved. The Gospels show me that Jesus felt the same way. Sometimes religion can sure get in the way of following Jesus and being spiritually-minded.

Have you ever been a part of "drive-by proselytizing" (as the recipient or the one talking)? How did that work out for you?

i don't know where to start

Other times, people don't share Jesus because they just don't know how to begin talking about Him. Imagine you are at Wendy's for lunch. "Would you like to Biggie-Size that?" they ask. You respond, "Not today. You know what God did in my life today?" Not a smooth segue at all. Where do you jump into this kind of conversation? What does that opportunity look like? Many leaders are talking about being "missional" these days, being purpose-driven, with a clear mission in sight. Great, I mostly agree. But where are you supposed to start? Or better yet, how are you supposed to start?

I like the way Saint Patrick started with the Celts, and I think it's a decent way to begin. His first move was obvious: go to the people. There is no way you can share what you have found in your relationship with Jesus unless you get around people. Next, Saint Patrick just lived around them. I'm fairly certain that you are already living around some people. A good move is to now learn from them. What's important to them? What makes them smile? What puzzles them? The important thing is to love the people you are around. Even if what they find important, pleasurable or puzzling is nothing like you. Love them.

I am convinced that you know people at work or next door or at the coffee shop that you are already doing all of this with. This is where Saint Patrick started, and soon he had introduced people in Ireland to the Jesus he knew, loved, and had been changed by. He did this by beginning his conversations about Jesus with what they knew, building on illustrations they understood. "I see you really dig the clover leaf. I like how the three leaves are joined into one leaf. That reminds me of God! Let me tell you why…"

Think of someone you know who doesn't know Jesus like you do. What are they into that you can use to explain what you have experienced with Jesus?

i don't know how people will react

A final reason that people retreat from sharing their faith is that they get freaked out over how others will react to the message. Using that same logic, it would follow that my mailman quits delivering my mail simply because he's not sure how I will take it. I've never gotten a bill in the mail or a letter with bad news and been ticked off at the U.S. Postal Service. All they do is deliver the message. That's what they are there for. The mailman isn't as concerned about my response as much as he is about doing the job he was hired to do.

As a follower of Jesus, I am entrusted with the job of sharing Jesus with others. I am expected to glow His glory. That's it. Just let the light of Christ be seen. For example: Lights do some pretty cool things with bugs. A single light will either draw or repel. Try it. Moths just flock to the light. Other bugs are indifferent to the presence of light. But roaches? They're another story. They run and hide. Flock or hide. Those are about the only responses I know to light, whether it's G.E. or J.C. Some people are drawn to Jesus when He is talked about, introduced, or demonstrated. Others pretty much don't acknowledge that anything is happening. Still others will run from the mention of Jesus. Their response to the Light shouldn't concern you as much as your obedience in shining that Light.

I know some Christians who have friends that don't follow Jesus simply so that they can introduce them to Jesus. That's really the only reason they hang out with them. I understand this to a point, but it can be so misleading. It's like using people's spiritual "unawareness," if you ask me. Jesus loved people first and foremost, and never looked at them as projects that He needed to complete. If they followed Him: great, an angel party was waiting to begin. And if they decided not to follow him: okay, but can we still have poker-night at your house tonight? The response of those around Him was never a condition of those He hung out with. He ate with tax-collectors, hookers, religious bigots, lepers, and only a few of those people are recorded as following Him at some point. Anything less than unconditional love and acceptance would have been a smokescreen that those groups would have seen right through.

I hate to converse with someone as a means to an end. I have friends who live in Nashville, The Music City, and I have acquaintances there. During one of my visits there, I was talking to this guy about why I wouldn't move there to work for Him. I figured I owed him an explanation of why I was rejecting the job he'd offered me. The job was great; it just wasn't what I knew God wanted me to be doing at that point. After I talked for a few minutes, he interrupted me and asked, "So what do you expect to gain from this conversation?" The man made six figures a year in the music industry, and was an executive at a record company. Yet, I felt so sorry for him. Were all the people he talked with expecting to gain something from a few words exchanged? How sad! Conversation is part of relationship. It's what opens our lives to one other. Conversation is what draws us into another person's life. That's important whether I get around to sharing Jesus or not.

Do you expect to gain something from the conversations you have with people? How would it make you feel if others expected to get something out of every chat with you?

practice makes perfect

The bottom line is that we have made too big of a production about what sharing our faith is. I don't think Jesus ever intended it to be this big of an ordeal. I don't remember Him mentioning that I had to memorize a 4-step plan, a 3-fold path, or a 12-step program to God through Jesus. Most of the stuff we use to share

Jesus wasn't even written until decades after He ascended into Heaven! Was He expecting us to wait for some good evangelism books to be written, or did He just want us to talk about what we knew? I think sharing Jesus with others was supposed to be a natural overflow of what was happening in our lives. Sharing our faith should just glow out of us. It is something we were told to practice. Yep: practice. That's what makes us get it right. (Is there even a wrong way?) We practice and practice so we can get better and better at it. Sharing our faith is not something that we study and debate in order to become experts before we engage in the activity. Did the disciples go to a weekend seminar to equip them? No. They just shared their Jesus encounters with other people. All they did was reflect the light God had placed in them. I wish we'd all just stop stressing out over the how-to's of talking to others about Jesus. We freeze up over not knowing the how-to's. They can also make us so busy that we never really get people together with Jesus.

All we are asked to do is to tell people about our experience with Jesus. We are not asked to "save" anybody. We can't do that. Only Jesus is a Savior. And we can't make anyone become a Christian. I believe the Holy Spirit is active in a person's life long before they accept Jesus' gift of salvation. My involvement in their spiritual journey is to join the Holy Spirit in making faith in Jesus real. My role is never to replace what the Holy Spirit is doing, or to pretend I am that person's personal Holy Spirit. I knew a girl who tried to be the Holy Spirit for me. She thought it was her personal responsibility to try to convict me of things she thought were wrong in my life. And she was way off base on some of her claims. I haven't talked to her for years, and a lot of it is a result of that terrible experience. She made a crappy Holy Spirit. And she's not alone. I make a crappy Holy Spirit, too. We all make crappy Holy Spirits. So why do so many of us think that part of sharing our faith is doing the Holy Spirit's job?

Here's an idea: just get Jesus and people together and let His power (not our activity or ability) heal the hurts and needs in our lives. When my daughter was three, I spent Father's Day in the ER with her because she fell down a couple of steps and broke her collar bone. There were a lot of tears, worry, and hope involved. The doctor said something to me that day that has stood out ever since. I asked if they needed to put a cast on Audrey. "Nope." the doc said, "Put two collar bones in a room together and they'll hook up and heal." Apparently, the collar bone is the easiest bone to break and the easiest bone to heal. No splint. No cast. No setting. They just grow back together without any sign of damage. Sometimes I think sharing Jesus with people is almost that easy. Just get broken people in a room with Jesus and they'll get together. Sure, that's probably oversimplifying things a bit. But is it really?

Jesus Christ, the Light of the World. That's a light that's hard to miss. But millions of people don't recognize Him. Maybe the problem is that sharing Jesus has become something we occasionally do and not something we always are.

Notice that most of the reasons we are afraid to talk about Jesus begin with the words "I don't know." Why are we so afraid of not knowing before we begin something?

Illustration Nº. 2 The Disco Bsll

a burning within reflecting out
chapter one

> For the Lord is the Spirit, and wherever the Spirit of the Lord is, there is freedom. So all of us who have had that veil removed can see and reflect the glory of the Lord. And the Lord—who is the Spirit—makes us more and more like him as we are changed into his glorious image.
> - The Apostle Paul in 2 Corinthians 3:17-18 (NLT)

I love these verses. Another translation says that we can be like mirrors that brightly reflect the glory of Lord. In many respects, these verses have become my purpose. Maybe more accurately and truthfully, they are only my goal. To be a mirror that brightly reflects the glory of the Lord is a great purpose in life. I desire that God be seen in me and the things I do. I want this so much more than making sure I myself am seen. When I am with my wife, I want to be a husband who desires to reflect the glory of the Lord.

I can reflect God and still be romantic. I don't take some celibate monk oath just because I want Jesus to be seen in my life. I can put on some Barry White and make out with her and still be a Jesus Follower who is reflecting godly love. When I'm playing with my daughters, I want God to be seen. I can be the goofy, funny, a big little kid while I demonstrate a serious relationship that altered my life. At work, I want to be a model employee and a reflection of God, having Him receive the glory, not me. Not just working for the man, but truly working for the Maker of all mankind. I'll still take the raise for my good job performance, and I may even increase my giving to the organizations and charities I support! What a wonderful and enduring purpose for those who follow Jesus: to pursue a life that reflects the glory of God like a mirror.

When do you feel like you are most reflecting Christ?

When do you feel like you are least reflective of Christ?

Now add to that the idea of being so bright, so like Christ, that all you can do is reflect His glory more and more. What an aspiration! What a goal! This has been my driving force for a few years now. That I continue to grow in my relationship with Christ in such a way the world around me cannot help but take notice. That I never get to a point of having enough when it comes to the things of God. I desire to be exposed to more and more of God so that His glory is seen. Glory is not ignored, especially God's glory.

The thing about the passage from the second letter to the church in Corinth is that it's so full of purpose. And it is for all of us. Really. Those words are right there: "all of us." What would the world be like if we all took this challenge to heart: to be like little mirrors that brightly reflect the glory of the Lord. How would our communities of faith change if the whole purpose of them was to grow to be like Him so we could reflect Him even more? What would the church look like?

the gospel discotheque

I think I know what this would look like. I think Chic, KC and The Sunshine Band, and the Bee Gees would love it! When I read 2 Corinthians 3:17-18, I see a disco ball. Go ahead, run to the retro clothing shop and grab a pair of bell bottoms and some big old platform shoes if you want; and make sure you have Saturday Night Fever in your Netflix queue. Welcome to Funkytown. But really, if we are all a bunch of mirrors fitted together in community for the sole purpose of reflecting the light of Christ to a dark world, I think it would totally be like a disco ball. We've all seen disco balls do their thing. One light shines on hundreds of little square mirrors, and two things happen. First, light is scattered in the darkness. In the early 90s I went to this concert with my friend, Todd. We saw The Smashing Pumpkins open up for Pearl Jam, who opened up for The Red Hot Chili Peppers; a killer night of rock and roll. We were seated safely in the balcony, watching this amoeba of flesh mosh around the floor. It was a great, safe perspective of a visual you have to experience to fully appreciate. When the Chili Peppers broke into their cover of Stevie Wonder's "Higher Ground," the disco ball kicked on, and that dark arena was lit up. The only light in the building was shining on a big three-foot disco ball, and illumination poured over the audience. That large auditorium was lit up by a single light on hundreds of mirrors.

As soon as that happened, a second thing occurred--laughter and dancing. Disco balls start parties. You can't help but feel good when the disco ball is in motion, with one flick of a switch, everyone around wants to be a part of the festivities. Joy and happiness and celebration run freely. At the Chili Peppers' show, the human amoeba was kicked into high gear. It looked like mayhem from where I was sitting. But I wanted to be there in the middle of it, basking in the adrenaline and sweat. People were jumping around, laughing and singing along. And I just stood and watched. I saw the party, but I wasn't an active part of it. I felt like a wallflower. Still, I could feel the party going on, and it made me smile. The next time I went to a show at that arena, I made sure I was on the floor in the midst of all the action, under the disco ball, ready to be part of the party and not just a spectator.

pointless disco balls

They may shine bright, but disco balls are needy. They need the darkness. A disco ball in a well-lit room is going to pretty much go unnoticed. In the same way, too many followers of Jesus are holed up in a well-lit room with their mirror buddies and mirror entertainment, going to mirror seminars put on by other mirrors about how to be shinier mirrors and what smudges to avoid. And the darkness is just getting darker. We cannot reflect His glory to His glory! We need darkness if the light is going to be seen. By contrast, a disco ball is also pointless unless there is light. We can't reflect our own dim glory, only the glory of the Lord. Our glory may turn some heads, but will rarely start a party. The common good of the community of mirrors is to reflect Jesus to a dark world. We need the light to survive.

Another element of pointless disco balls is one that is not in motion. It may reflect the light without spinning around, but it is not near reaching its potential. As a community of followers of Christ, we must be in motion. We cannot just take the gifts God gives us and sit down. We must use them. Put motion to the movement, the revolution of following Jesus.

Darkness and motion are necessary to make the reflection of a disco ball more effective. If you were a mirror on a disco ball, how effective do you think you'd be?

I've noticed one other interesting thing about disco balls. The closer the light gets to the mirrors, the greater the reflective light. Pull the light away and the impact on a dark room subsides. But place that light closer, and watch it glare.

Biblically, I think this is illustrated by what occurred on the road to Emmaus shortly after the resurrection of Jesus. You can read about it in the book of Luke, Chapter 24. A couple days after Jesus defied death by rising up from the dead; these two guys were walking down a road that leads to a little village called Emmaus, just outside of Jerusalem. Only one of the guys' names is mentioned, Cleopas. (God must think that the 'what' of the event mattered more than the 'who', because I really doubt He ever forgets people's names!) After events like the ones they experienced the weekend before, their conversation was pretty focused. "Dude, He was dead, then gone?" "Where's a dead body gonna' go?" "Um, didn't Jesus say He was going to bring a new kingdom to us? How? By dying?!" All of a sudden, this other guy shows up and joins both the conversation and journey. It was Jesus, but the two social commentators didn't realize it was Him, yet.

Jesus says, "You guys seem like you are talking about something pretty serious. What's the big deal? What's going on? Did I miss something?"

Their pace was halted. Despair, confusion, betrayal, and sadness were written across their faces. "What rock have you been under?" Cleopas asks. "Don't you know what's been going on in Jerusalem since Friday?"

"Like what?" Jesus asks.

"Like what happened to the man named Jesus. Remember? Come on; you've heard of Him, right? That carpenter from Nazareth! He was this prophet who did these way cool tricks and miracles."

"Oh! And could that guy ever teach. He'd make the most profound statements about life and stuff, using whatever objects were around or making up these little stories that I didn't always get, but always thought were so awesome."

"Everybody except the pastors around town liked the guy, I suppose. They hated Him so much that they had Him arrested, lied about Him in the quickest court sessions I've ever heard of, and then crucified Him. It sucked!"

"Man, we really thought He was God's Promised One who'd take us out of here. You know, the Messiah who's going to rescue all of Israel. But first He goes and dies, and then a few days ago, this other bizarre thing happens. These ladies go to the cemetery on Sunday to give Him flowers and stuff, and they come back saying He's risen from the dead! That His body is not in the grave, and these angels told them Jesus was alive. A couple of friends of ours are totally not buying this, so they run to the cemetery. Sure enough, the ladies were right. He's gone, or alive, or something. Why do all these other people get to know for sure? If I'm going to buy it, I want to see Him myself!"

Then Jesus interrupts, "Come on you two. You know better than this. Didn't the prophets talk about this in all of those Sabbath School stories you were taught? Didn't they all say that the Messiah would have to do all this stuff you just said?" Then Jesus quotes all those passages from the prophets about the Messiah and explains them to the guys on the road to Emmaus. Talks about Himself, really, pointing out all the places the Messiah was throughout the Scriptures. But Cleopas and his friend still don't realize who they are hiking with.

Finally, their seven-mile walk and mobile classroom is just about over. Jesus says, "Later," and starts to go on. But the guys say it's too late and that He needs to eat dinner anyway, so they invite Him over for a cookout. So Jesus goes over, and when it's time to eat, Jesus takes a hamburger bun and asks God's blessing on it, breaks it up, and gives it to each of them. "Oh! Oh! Oh! That's just like Jesus did the other night when …" Poof! Jesus disappears. Then they get it. It was Jesus they were with.

Then they say the coolest thing. "Didn't our heats burn within us (or feel strangely warm) as He talked with us on the road and explained Scriptures to us?"

So they're off! They book it back the entire seven-mile walk to Jerusalem to tell the 11 disciples and all the other followers of Jesus what happened to them. "Hey! We saw Jesus for ourselves." "I know," they say. "Peter just saw the risen Lord, too." But Cleopas and his friend had a great story to tell, so they were probably up all night talking about their awesome day with a formerly dead man.

Imagine what that would have been like. What a great experience, to walk and talk with a risen Lord. To have that close company with Him. To discuss what's on your mind, hear from His heart, and then have the opportunity to tell your friend about what you just experienced. Think about what it would have been like to spend that time so close to the Light of the World. I'd cherish that moment. I'd want to talk about it, too. I don't think I'd ever be the same.

Read Luke 24:13-35 for yourself. When have you felt like the two guys on the way to Emmaus? When, after a time with Jesus, you felt like you were glowing …

e.t. and Jesus

We read in verse 32, "didn't our hearts feel strangely warm as He talked with us," or in another translation, "did not our hearts burn within us?" That's the result of a light getting closer to the mirrors. When I read about these two guys, I can't help but think of E.T. Yes, that E.T., the alien that Drew Barrymore freaked out about and fed Reese's Pieces to. E.T. had a burning within, a glow.

Close to the end of the movie, Elliott is doing better, but only because E.T. gave up his life so Elliott could live. Elliott goes into the chamber that houses the pod containing E.T.'s poor little anemic, lifeless, alien body, to say goodbye to his new friend from outer space. As he is leaving, he notices a few flowers are coming back to life without the help of Miracle Grow. Elliott rushes back into the chamber, and there he sees a resurrected, glowing E.T. He's glowing! And he continues to glow until he is finally able to "go home."

His little alien belly lit up. It glowed. I doubt these two guys on the road to Emmaus had an external reaction like E.T.'s glow. There were no Reese's Pieces involved. And I know they didn't fly bicycles over a moon-lit sky. "Did not our hearts burn within us?" they said. Their glowing within was reflecting out. It was never turned into a Steven Spielberg blockbuster, but I bet the experience at Emmaus was just as memorable.

the perfect fire

We, too, should seek out that internal glow that we only get by our time in the presence of Jesus. The idea of a glow is like the embers of a fireplace, not flames. A few years back, I was at this youth retreat, and a fireman friend of mine named Michael built the biggest bonfire I have ever seen. I hope I never see a bonfire like that again. You could've roasted marshmallows from a hundred feet away! There was no getting close to that fire. It hurt. It was too hot, too dangerous. It was far from a perfect bonfire. It was indeed a killer fire, but it defeated the purpose. Once that fire cooled down (a day later), the embers were just right to warm yourself by without the risk of hospitalization.

I've stoked a fire before. And when there are constant embers (like when they are glowing), the rekindling of the fire happens easily when more wood is thrown on it. You can roast hotdogs on this fire. It's a S'mores sort of fire. The sing-a-long songs and ghost stories are just moments away when the fire is fueled, not by flames, but by glowing embers that create the perfect fire. That's so much more useful to everyone than a bonfire with flames out of control.

Our hearts need rekindling. A.W. Tozer noted that at one time we were expecting from God, but now we have just settled to merely say nice things about Him; once, we expected miracles from Him, but now we doubt. (Maybe it's because we are too "realistic.") As Tozer put it, "Once, we were thrilled, and now we are chilled." We could all definitely use some spiritual stoking, bringing the thrill back to our relationship with Jesus, to be poked and prodded by the Holy Spirit to warm us up, so that our hearts may burn within us. To stir up that light that we so often find buried beneath our everyday living.

The light that we have within us has a purpose. Isaiah said that God would do more than just restore the people to Himself; that He would make each one of us a light to the world. Each believer is a tool to bring salvation to the whole world. This is no easy task, as the world seems to get darker and darker and our glow seems to get dimmer and dimmer. To get us going in the right direction, the Apostle Paul, in

Philippians, wrote that we are to live clean and innocent lives just like a little kid. This is what's expected of Jesus followers in a world full of crooked and perverse people following their own desires. The reason for this is so that we can let our lives "shine brightly before them." To become a light in the darkness that naturally reflects the Light of the World.

Did you get the point of our glow here? The purpose of this little light of mine is to impact the world, not my church or my Christian friends. Without the darkness, a disco ball will look pretty stupid. Without the light, there is no reflection. Without the reflection, there can be no party. How are you doing as a mirror of His glory? Is your heart "burning within you?"

I have an idea of what the burning was. Perhaps it was a reflection within, glowing out. Those two guys on their way to Emmaus were just two human mirrors that spent time with Jesus, and the result was a glow they couldn't hold back. Immediately, they had to go tell their friends what they experienced. I bet the moment they walked in the room the disciples knew something was up. You can always tell when someone has good news for you. Their faces are a dead giveaway that something is up. And that something is really good news you can't wait to hear.

Each one of us has the Good News. Can those around you tell? How's your glow?

this little light of mine

Kids' songs tick me off. Sometimes the simple lyrics and melodies that we teach our children are too convicting to the parents. I wonder if the kids' song writers know this when they write these tunes. "Okay, not too many words here. We want the kids to sing them over and over until their parents get the point." They seem so innocent, that is until I start to pay attention to what they are really saying.

Ever since I was a little kid in Sunday School, or even just hanging out at grandma's house, I've been singing "This Little Light of Mine." Oh, yes. "I'm gonna let it shine," "Hide it under a bushel? NO!" and "Let it shine 'til Jesus comes." You probably know the song. It's a great song and not just for the kids. This little children's classic from years past has a serious implication that deserves to be looked at: we may be shining, but how bright? How effective is the illumination this little light is giving off? Ouch. And why is it just a "little" light? Am I afraid to let it be a bigger one? Am I hiding it under a bushel? I haven't been around any bushels lately, so could I be hiding the little light under anything else? Rather than the emphatic "NO!" we shouted and sang as children, when we honestly assess the implications as adults, we would at best say, "Well, maybe most of the time." But that phrasing doesn't fit the song. This little song is full of conviction for those of us who fail to glow with our whole being. Even the honest "most of the time" reality is tough to achieve sometimes.

Another implication to consider: we may be glowing, but where? Is it just in our comfy community of believers, or are we shining to a world that needs the Light of Christ? I have yet to see an essential light when light already exists. You don't use a flashlight on a sunny day, only at night. Why flip on a desk lamp when the window nearby is letting the sun's rays beam right in next to you? In all my illumination experience, I've found that light is most effective when shining in the darkness. Sometimes the darkness is even necessary in order for the light to be seen at all.

in and excluded from?

This is an area of much misunderstanding in the church. One little biblical phrase has set the church at odds with the world, separating the light from the darkness. Four words out of the multitude of words in the Bible have created picketing, boycotting, a few bombings, some vandalism, and probably a few wars. That phrase? "In, but not of." We've all heard it, maybe even recited it. But have we understood it? It's not a separation thing. It's not a call to exclude the world; but, rather, a call to influence those around us that may be oblivious to the light of Christ. Not to force others to conform, but to transform the world around us through introducing others to the character of Jesus Christ.

Read John 17:14-15. How do you balance the idea of "in the world but not of it?"

Read Romans 12:2-9. What do these verses have to do with being "in the world but not of it?"

The thing is that it can be difficult finding a balance between our spirituality and the world we live in. The two are so different. How can we be other-worldly in a world so worldly? How can I be a Christian when everything around me is so not Christian? Finding that middle ground is the whole point of our call to be "in the world but not of it"; it can be a struggle to find the balance. I want to be spiritual and influence those around me with the Truth that has been revealed to me. But I also work at a job, eat in restaurants, shop in stores, watch movies, and listen to music that has no respect for what I believe in my heart.

the life of a pharisee

This struggle to find some sort of cultural balance is not new. The Bible talks about four distinct groups of people who had a hard time balancing the gospel with the culture. First there were the Pharisees. Jesus' strongest words were reserved for these religious leaders who professed truth with their mouths but denied the essence of that truth by the way they were living. It wasn't their denominational stance or church growth strategies that ticked Jesus off. It was a huge ivory chip on their shoulders that was primarily self-exalting. The Pharisees were so set on obeying all 613 Old Testament laws that they pretty much sat back, judged their culture, and attempted to remove culture from everybody else. These men truly loved the law of the Lord. They just went to some pretty harsh extremes in upholding it for themselves and forcing others to uphold it as well. And when other Jews didn't practice religion as hard-core as they did, the Pharisees wouldn't hang out with them. These guys found every part of the social culture they didn't like and then used the Law to make it out to be wrong in God's eyes. No matter how noble the motive, if the action was not according to the Law, then it was flat out wrong. Even if it was healing at the wrong time, talking with the wrong race, or loving the rejects of society; if what was done was contrary to the ancient law of the Israelites, the Pharisees frowned upon it and condemned the ones in action. So when Jesus showed up, the very eyes, hands and feet of God found themselves firmly placed in the culture that the Pharisees despised. One time Jesus told them that they were like whitewashed tombs, all pretty and white on the outside, but decaying, rotting, and stinking to high heaven on the inside.

You see, when you begin despising the world you live in, you lose the burden and compassionate heart for the world you live in. I may not agree with everything going on around me, but I am to reach out a helping hand to those that Jesus would have. That means "the least of these" (see Matthew 25:34-45.) No one is attracted to a self-righteous, judgmental attitude. Plus, it's a slippery slope to begin pointing out what God dislikes in others. I remember Jesus saying it can be like looking for a speck of dust in my neighbor's eye while I have a fence post sticking out of my own. The Pharisees were out of balance because they placed so much emphasis on their spirituality that they hated the culture around them. We all know some Pharisees, don't we?

the life of a sadducee

Then there were the Sadducees. These were the wealthy ones, born into the high rank of culture. Aristocrats. The Sadducees were the most powerful members of the priesthood. These guys liked the clout and status they had within society. So, in an effort to maintain their standing, they tended to weaken the laws Moses handed down. If the standard is lowered, it's a lot easier to achieve.

I see a lot of people weakening the gospel in order to appeal to people. I see a whole movement within the Church that so wants to use culture to introduce people to Jesus that they tend to weaken the Message of the Bible in an effort to remain relevant. Brian McLaren and Tony Campolo have gone as far as to say that much of the modern Christian church has "neutered the gospel." We've taken the offensive stuff out so people won't be put off by it.

the life of a zealot

Next were the Zealots. They were pretty much fanatical Pharisees who took the upholding of the Law to some severe ends. These people thought they could change culture by changing or rebelling against laws and politics. My dad ran for state Senate when I was in college. Dad really wanted to see people in our city and state change for the better, but he also realized that sometimes making a difference is more important than making changes. He lost the bid, but his campaign slogan was great: "Conformation through transformation." My dad was smart enough to realize that laws will never change people's hearts. They need the transforming touch of Christ that makes them new creatures, not just law-abiding ones. Zealots use political platforms and lobbying to try to change culture into what their convictions hold. They "vote" their morality on others.

The trouble with this is that spirituality is a matter of the heart, not popular opinion. A majority vote does not a godly people make. I am all for Christ followers being involved in politics; but as a means of influence, not of bullying power. I think that too often politicians and lobbying groups use their religion to gain a vote, not grow the Kingdom of God. One's spirituality should never move one to political extremes that basically find no home in any viewpoint but their own.

the life of an essene

Finally, the Bible mentions the Essenes. These Jewish people were disciplined, even stricter than the Pharisees. But the Essenes were so disciplined that they totally removed themselves from culture, opting to just hang out by themselves. They were their own people, living a communal life. If they didn't agree with you or your viewpoints, they could not hang out with you at all. "Who needs ya' if you don't believe the way we do!"

Many people are part of a Christian subculture in America. They read only Christian books, watch only Christian TV, listen only to Christian radio, and eat only at restaurants that are owned by Christians.
The 80s new-wave rocker, Steve Taylor, quipped that they "only drink milk from Christian cows." Worldly

culture is viewed as so depraved and far gone that they must fully remove themselves from it. Only have Christian friends. Only do business with Christian business people. It's a limited sphere of influence to be sure. If I reject glowing in the areas I disagree with, the whole point of having a glow is defeated.

Pharisee, Sadducee, Zealot, Essene. We've all encountered people like this. Rather than identify these people in others, which one would you say is most identifiable in you? Why?

in but not of

Light needs darkness to be effective, but it needs to remain the light. A pastor friend of mine said to think of being in a boat on the middle of a big lake. As long as I am resting in that boat, I can say I am "in the lake." A friend calls my cell and asks where I am. "I'm in the middle of Lake Tahoe." As soon as I jump out of that boat, I am "of the lake." It's the same with the world. I can still go to movies, listen to the radio, eat at restaurants that serve beer, support public schools, and go to art shows. I can do all of this and still follow Jesus. I really don't think Jesus would hang exclusively at our churches and cathedrals if He were tooling around the world today. We'd probably kick Him out for being too radical anyway. As Todd Agnew sings, "He'd prefer Beale Street to the stained-glass crowd." He'd be at the bars, the art galleries and coffee shops, NAACP meetings and public school theater productions. Places where He could make a difference, not places He would just blend into. He wouldn't necessarily love all the ideals, opinions, and agendas that are part of these gatherings, but He would undeniably love the people who were a part of them. He'd be in the world, not of it.

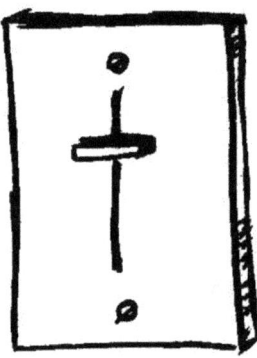

Illustration No. 3 The Dimmer Switch

what keeps us from shinning bright?
chapter two

Look at 2 Corinthians 3:17-18 again.

> For the Lord is the Spirit, and wherever the Spirit of the Lord is, there is freedom. So all of us who have had that veil removed can see and reflect the glory of the Lord. And the Lord—who is the Spirit—makes us more and more like him as we are changed into his glorious image. (NLT)

This is a guide for us. If we were "perfectly reflecting the glory of the Lord," we could not be missed!! That's the whole point of glowing: to expose the darkness with His light. For too long, the community of faith has sat in one room and complained about the world in the other room. We have a party upstairs, and condemn to the basement of hell the ones who don't follow Jesus. Without the influence of people reflecting Jesus Christ, the world will only get darker and darker. A dirty room looks pretty clean with the lights off. Rooms look dust free until the lights come on.

I love to see bi-vocational ministers; men and women who may shepherd a flock, but are also actively involved in the workplace. At least they are out in the community. Years ago, Rick Warren wrote a book called The Purpose Driven Life. Maybe you read it. One of the things that Rick Warren's Purpose Driven book so clearly states is that we are all ministers of Jesus. We can't just follow Him and let that be it. It is one of my purposes to utilize what God has given me to draw people into relationship with Him. In a way, the people I work with, live around, and sit by at the soccer games are the sheep God has entrusted me to shepherd. This is called ministry. And if the only place I minister is in my church or with other Jesus followers, I am wasting my purpose.

I can't begin a relationship with my wife and daughters. I am already a part of that family. Don't bother introducing me to my wife or talking about how beautiful she is; and there's no need to tell me all about how infectious the smile, joy and laughter of my daughter is. I know. I live there. It's obvious to me. So why do we spend so much of our time, energy, and resources on drawing people in our churches into relationships they already have with Jesus?! It's redundant. Start something new. Create a revolution. Invite people to join the family, so to speak. Let your neighbor in on the relationship with Jesus, even if your neighbor is gay. Tell your coworker about the difference Jesus made in your life, even if she's an alcoholic. You know, we need to glow, reflect, and shine Jesus to the world because they are gay, alcoholic, sleep around a lot, have lost hope, worship money or love pornos!

city on a hill

Jesus said in Matthew 5:14-16, that we are the light of the world. He said He wants us to be like a city on a hill at night: you can't miss it because it just glows. Then He goes deeper and says we need to quit hiding the fact that we glow; but instead we need to display that light of mine, no matter how little. And maybe a good place to start isn't with some street-evangelism effort that will get us only a few looks, some snide comments, and two sore feet. The best place to start being the light of the world is wherever good deeds are needed. Again, the point is not to make us look good, but to make others see Jesus in us.

I do not sense any indication that Jesus expected us to seclude our light; but, rather we should let others see it in a dark world. Do I know my neighborhood bartender? How about the guy who goes there every night to escape his pain? Have I really asked that girl at the coffee shop how my family can help her and her son out since her boyfriend left her? When the homosexual couple down the street had that fire, did I offer any help? That Muslim family doesn't have a mower right now; why didn't I mow their lawn? Usually we answer these questions with the excuse that we don't want to promote their lifestyle by assisting them in their path away from God. Well, how will they ever see the beacon light of Jesus without me doing my part? Without accepting my responsibility as a follower of Jesus to minister to them the way He would? It's my purpose to embrace the people in my world of influence in a way that allows the Holy Spirit of God to shine into their world. It's my responsibility to love the people in my world, regardless of their sins. It's my responsibility to be active in the world but of Jesus.

dimmer switches

The same electricity that flows through a spotlight at a concert flows through the floor lamp by my chair.

Flip a switch on the wall to light a room, and the same electricity illuminates my nightlight. These things have different purposes, and thus, different shining power. But they all have the same power source. When it comes to the light that supplies our glow, we all have the same power source. Looking at the illustration of the whole disco ball thing, Jesus' light is reflected through us; the same power source illuminating. But those thousand little mirrors do not all reflect in the same way. They shoot light into different areas of a room. Different people are created differently, have different gifts from God, and different purposes and callings. We each glow differently than others, namely because we are different than others. To expect the same exact glow out of each one who follows Christ is to deny His creativity in creation.

The variation comes in how well we shine where and how God wants us to. Some rooms' lights have dimmer switches that distort the flow of electricity, allowing us to increase or decrease the brightness of a light. How bright we shine and how well we glow is up to our control of similar dimmer switches. So what are some of these dimmer switches that we need to be aware of?

not talking

Not talking dims our glow, too. Please don't think I am a moron. I know we talk. We talk all day long. With friends and with strangers, communication happens. Cell phones, wireless networks, Facebook, Twitter, coffee shops, and dinner tables are Petri-dishes of communication experiments. We want to know the who-what-where-when-why-how stuff of life. The issue isn't if we talk, but rather what we talk about. In all of this conversation, when do you use words like "Here's what God's doing in my life?" "My faith in Jesus really kicked in when I went through my divorce. How are you getting through yours?" "I was an addict, too. Can I tell you how Jesus helped me out of that lifestyle?" "Am I spiritual? I guess you could say that. But my relationship with Jesus goes a lot deeper. Can I tell you about it?" "Dude, I am so sorry to hear that. I wish I could fix it for you, but can I pray with you right now?" When we neglect saying things like this at all, we put dimmers on our glow.

We cannot expect to live life with only spiritual conversations taking place, basing every word on our relationship with and the person of Christ. But we are expected to talk about Him with those who believe and those who have yet to believe. Peter said in Acts 4:20 that there was no way he could even stop talking about all of the cool stuff God was doing in his life. Try to shut him up about it! There was too much to say, so Peter just kept on talking, even though they put him in jail and crucified him upside down.

This guy was never concerned with not talking. God was doing so many cool things in his life that he just had to tell others about it. I bet a trip to McDonald's with Peter would turn into an evangelism opportunity. I have a friend who does inner city ministry in Washington D.C. who has this ability. Literally, anywhere Chris goes he will initiate spiritual conversations by talking about his spiritual life to perfect strangers. It's awesome! We went to Arby's one time, and before we left, he'd talked about Jesus with like three people other than me. When Chris talks about the things he's recently discovered about God or life with him, Chris glows the light of Jesus to those around him. And it's natural. It doesn't come across cheesy, but authentic. When I just sit in silent amazement and astonished wonder at this rare ability, I fail to glow.

"What has God done in your life that you wish everyone knew about?"

going with the grain

Another dimmer switch that negatively affects our glow is going with the grain. I don't care if you are in jr. high or in the workplace, peer pressure affects us all. What others think of us is seldom something we don't care about. When it comes to glowing, it's easy to dim our glow for acceptance. Religious nut. Goody two shoes. Holy roller. Jesus Freak. Just a plain old Freak. Prude. The list could go on for miles; people have opinions of people with a spiritual focus. They include our families, our friends, and our neighbors. We have to live with them, see them across the fence, and work side by side. What they think of us affects us. But more important is how we let what they think of us affect how well we glow. "We serve God whether people honor us or despise us, whether they slander us or praise us," writes Paul in 2 Corinthians 6:8-10.

> We serve God whether people honor us or despise us, whether they slander us or praise us. We are honest, but they call us impostors. We are well-known, but we are treated as unknown. We live close to death, but here we are, still alive. We have been beaten within an inch of our lives. Our hearts ache, but we always have joy. We are poor, but we give spiritual riches to others. We own nothing, and yet we have everything. (NLT)

Or, for an Old Testament example, look at Shadrach, Meshach, and Abednego. These guys wouldn't bow to the status quo and they were thrown in the fire. Talk about against the grain!

Read the story of Shadrach, Meshach, and Abednego in Daniel 3. How would you handle the pressure of this situation?

Holding up under that kind of pressure is tough. Not that we have ever had to deal with persecution that intense. We are asked to put our Bible away at work or quit humming "Amazing Grace," and we think we're being persecuted. There are people in China who are killed for owning a page of the Bible, and we complain that we don't have a place to put a pen in our Bible cover with interchangeable handles. People in Nepal are killed for teaching the Word to their children, and we get embarrassed when our kids sing "Every Move I Make" loudly at The Gap. We've never tasted persecution, and yet we let our glow dim just to fit in … or at least so we don't have to deal with looks and stares from others. We would buckle so quickly and so badly if we had to face the kind of persecution that the early church did. Every time we hold back, and every time we quit talking or singing just because someone else is around, we dim our glow.

denying the Light

When I was a sophomore in high school, I learned a valuable lesson in denial. I'm a PK, a pastor's kid. Both of my parents served in a church in Des Moines, Iowa, for nearly three decades. One time, when the whole, "What's your dad do?" conversation began before my geometry class, my solid, foundational upbringing in the church gave me the strength to proclaim, "My dad's a pastor, but you couldn't tell, could you?" The next hour was the worst one of my schooling. "Theorem-blah-blah-blah-loser-x equals-blah-blah-backstabber-embarrassment to the faith-blah-blah" was all I heard in my head. I can't believe I did that. It couldn't have been me. You can bet that whatever glow I may have had was doused by the waters of my denial at this point.

"Me? A Christian? What do you think?" I hope you never have to go through the pains of uttering those words. They aren't bad words; they just deny any affirmation of a relationship with God, leaving speculation to determine any convictions. But convictions are spoken, not assumed. At least I was in good company with my denial.

In John 18, Peter full-on denies knowing Christ. He looks a dying Jesus in the face, and says he doesn't know who Jesus is. Whoa. Any embers in Peter's life must've been doused at that point. Peter is not a standard for us. It's not an example that if you want to introduce a section of the world to Jesus, then you should start by denying him. This is a good bad example of what not to do. I know that feeling. I recognize the scent of the smoke from that snuffed flame. But there is hope when we dim our glow out of denial. In Acts 2, just a few weeks after the big denial, Peter preaches a very pointed sermon which results in over 2,000 people deciding to be Jesus followers. Now that's some glowing!

Have you or someone close to you ever denied having a relationship with Jesus? How did that make you feel?

sin

I recently cleaned a light globe in my daughter's room that hadn't been cleaned for months. Okay, it had been a year. It was dusty and had few dead bugs in it. It was nasty. An amazing thing happened after I washed it and put it back up: the light was suddenly brighter in her room! I know that no scientific experiments need to take place to figure out why. Dirt and grime get in the way of keeping things clean and clear. Just a little dirt makes a bottle of water undrinkable. In the same way, our glow is affected by the presence of sin.

1 John 1:8 says that if I say I'm free from sin, then I am a liar. I'm fooling myself and denying the Truth that I know. When Paul wrote that "all have sinned," that included you and me. There are years of my life that would illustrate that I am an expert at sinning. Recently, God did some deep cleaning in my life and exposed in me the worst sins that I had no idea I even had. Had you asked me on Monday if I was guilty of the sins God exposed on Tuesday, I'd have thought you were a loon. But sure enough, there it was. And is. I can find some sin in my life without looking too hard.

Sin. It's such a dirty word, really. There's absolutely nothing compelling or complementary about those three letters combined in a way that defines our natural state. We have a tendency to excuse it by thinking, "It's not sin, it's a 'struggle area,'" or "What can I say?; it's just human nature." Yep. Exactly. It is human nature, and it's called sin.

"Don't be fooled by those who try to excuse these sins, for the anger of God will fall on all who disobey him." That's what it says in Ephesians 5:6. Sin is sin, and there really is no excusing it.

Why do we try to excuse our sin? What makes sin more attractive than the absence of it?

I know a guy that loves God, but loves his sin more. Even when a moment is before him to seek redemption, he will seek his sin first. He goes to church, raises his hands in worship, prays, reads the Bible, and the whole thing. But he is a blatant sinner, drunk on the weekends, swearing like a sailor, and sleeping with his girlfriend as often as he can. He doesn't pretend any different to those he's around. How does this reflect the light of Christ to those around him? If anything is said about Jesus in this guy's life, it is that he makes no difference in a person's life. His glow has been blown out, not just dimmed. Nothing douses a glowing ember like sin.

not sharing your faith

Not rising to the occasion dims our glow, too. I've said it before, and I'm saying it again. My name is Randy. (Hi, Randy!) And I hate witnessing. When it comes to sharing my faith, nothing makes my palms sweatier or my stomach ache quicker. Witnessing is not easy for many of us. I've never read any of Jesus' words that let us off the hook, though. At the end of His earthly ministry, He did not give a Great Suggestion, but a Great Commission, one that most of us turn into the Great Omission. Paul was killer at witnessing. My favorite example of how great he was at sharing his faith is in Acts 17:22-34.

So this one day Paul is strolling around Athens, and gets invited to speak to all the philosophers at this place called Mars Hill. He gets up in front of them and says, "Hey guys! I can tell you are very religious people. You have altars, shrines, and gods for just about everything all over the place. And just to make sure you are good with all the gods you worship and not accidentally miss any, you even have an altar and idol with this engraved on it: 'To the unknown God.' That's pretty cool! You've been worshipping my God without even knowing it, and today I am going to tell you about Him!"

Paul goes on to tell them about how God made the world and everything in it, so the philosophers' study of metaphysics could stop with Yahweh God. He tells them to quit building all the altars and making goofy sacrifices, since God doesn't live in a temple; that he is so beyond that and doesn't need their help with food and stuff. Paul tells these philosophers, people that most of us would run from, the facts that God is the very air we breathe and that He satisfies every need we could ever have, pretty much as easily as breathing is for us. He tells them about the creation of the world and about the plan that God has for this world He created. They are told that everything God does, He does for one reason, to help people find their way to Him. "But He's not hiding or anything!" Paul said. "He's not far from any one of us. If you are living, existing or moving, then God is involved right there!" Then Paul quotes a pagan poet who said we are the offspring of God. And as such, we really shouldn't limit God to an idol made out of wood, gold or whatever. After all, God made the craftsmen. "Oh! God's not ticked off at you for missing the point," Paul assures them. "He won't hold it against you, but you do need to turn away from all of your idols and turn toward Him." Finally, Paul wraps up his sermon with the reality of a judgment day that we all must face at some point.

I love the next part.

> When they heard Paul speak of the resurrection of the dead, some laughed in contempt, but others said, "We want to hear more about this later." That ended Paul's discussion with them, but some joined him and became believers. Among them were Dionysus, a member of the Council, a woman named Damaris, and others with them. (NLT)

Wow! How cool would it be to have that kind of impact? To glow Jesus so much that people are drawn to His light? That's what Jesus commanded us to do when He said to "go into all the world and make disciples in His name." We can do this. He's commissioned us to do it. He's equipped us to do it. So why don't we?

We can always find an excuse, usually sounding something like, "Well, I don't want to offend anyone." I heard a pastor say that when we fail to share our faith, we are pretty much telling someone to "go to hell." Their eternal future is at our fingertips, and we don't want to offend. What's more offensive than "you can go to hell!" This attitude will definitely dim our glow!

In an episode of Seinfeld, Elaine is dating a guy named Putty, who's a Christian, but he never talks about it. When asked why he doesn't, he says, "Why should I? You're the one going to hell, not me." Do you think this portrayal is accurate of most people who follow Jesus? Why?

ignoring the needs of others

One last way dimmer switches weaken our glows is when we ignore the needs of others. The bottom line is that if we love God, then we love others. One follows the other. You can't leave one out; they both have to be present. There's no, "This isn't a good idea," or, "Maybe I'll love her, but not him" stuff. It's not either/or. It's both/and. Jesus took this issue pretty seriously in Luke 10:25-37. Maybe you've heard the story he told.

There was this Jewish guy walking from Jerusalem to Jericho. It's really not that great of a walk. No cool scenery or little places to stop for a cup of coffee. Anyway, as he's on his journey, these bandits jump him. He must have had some sweet clothes on, because they ripped them off. They took his iPod, all of his money, and credit cards too. He was in way bad shape, lying on the side of the road half dead.

It just so happened that this Jewish priest was walking by and saw him laying there. Obviously this man needed some help. A bleeding dude in his boxers is a pretty clear indication that something may be awry. "I'm a priest, not a doctor!" But he must have had some pretty important church business to attend to, because he went to the other side of the street to avoid the guy.

A little while later, a worship leader from some church goes strolling by, surely listening to the latest worship CD and thinking about what songs he should use on Sunday morning. But with the guitar and a whole worship team waiting to practice at the church, he had to cross the street to avoid the guy as well.

Then this Samaritan walks by. The beat up guy and this guy were enemies. It'd be like an Iraqi rebel and a Marine meeting one another on the street, and one of them needing some help. So much for any amount of hope for the wounded, right? But instead of kicking the Jewish man when he was down, the Bible says the Samaritan "felt deep pity." This guy takes his enemy, cleans and covers his wounds, puts him in his ride, and drives him to the Hilton Suites so that he has a safe place to stay. Then he orders room service and a couple of movies for the Jew while he regains his strength.

The next day, the Samaritan goes to the front desk and puts it all on his Visa. "Make sure they guy in 1030 is taken care of. And call a doctor in to look him over. I'll take care of whatever costs may be incurred for the guy for the rest of the week, too. Just let me know how much I owe you." He didn't even ask the Jewish guy for a dime!!

"Now, which of these three would you say was a neighbor to the man who was attacked by bandits? Was it the priest, the worship leader, or the Samaritan?" Jesus asked. The man Jesus was telling this story to replied, "The one who showed him mercy." Then Jesus once again raised the bar for all of us. "You are so right! Now go and do the same." This wasn't a one-time deal for Jesus, but something He expects His followers to do often.

Thankfully, few of us are like the priest. He's a jerk in this story; avoiding the situation all together. (This is no reflection of clergy as a whole. I know plenty of cool priests.) The worship leader wasn't any less of a jerk, basically rubber-necking, but offering no assistance. But few of us are like the Samaritan. Few of us would stop, let alone sacrifice for the sake of a stranded stranger. Now, I know that sometimes helping the one by the side of the road is risky. People play sick tricks, and precaution is necessary. But it's no excuse for ignoring the needs of our neighbors. We are supposed to shine in the darkness without fear.

1 John 1:5-6 says that we have been given the message of Good News for the purpose of announcing it to others. And the message is really simple: "God is light and there is no darkness in him at all." Then the Bible says we are liars if we claim to be God followers but live without His light affecting us. I can't be surrounded by darkness if I'm supposed to have a light glowing inside of me. When this happens, I may be living, but I'm living a lie.

Remember: the light needs to overtake the darkness, removing all fear and worry about the what-may-bes. When we don't reach out, when we ignore the needs of others, we dim our glow.

We can look further than the one stranded on the side of the road. There are other ways we can glow by reaching out to those in need. When was the last time you served your community at a non-profit fund-raising event? You and your family could walk in the "Light the Night" fundraiser for Leukemia each year. It is one night and a couple hundred dollars; not much to pay for a great cause. How about volunteering one Saturday a month at a local mission? Joining the PTA or Big Brothers Big Sisters are great chances to glow, too. I have a friend, who in an effort to reach out and meet needs of others, does all the janitorial work for a church that he doesn't even attend. My friend Rob's church has been going to an inner city park on Sundays, cooking hundreds of burgers and hot-dogs just to give to the people at the park, including hookers, pimps, dealers, junkies, and gang members. The church members play basketball, hang out, and play with the kids at the playground. They even started a Sunday School of sorts for the kids. One guy I know takes less fortunate people from his recovery group to the local Christian bookstore and buys them stuff he hears them say would be cool to have.

Maybe you can share your glow with others by stopping at the old-folks home and listening to the stories of the tenants for a few minutes. The joy of your attention is what you bring these people. Maybe it's cleaning up a mile of highway with your small group. You see the signs while you are driving; why not get your church's name on there and do your part? Maybe it's doing your part for Big-Brothers, Big-Sisters. Maybe it's organizing a benefit concert for a ministry to unwed mothers, or writing a check to World Vision. Perhaps it's forfeiting a venti non-fat caramel machiatto for the sake of The Mocha Club. Why not direct people's attention and the attention of the political arena to theonecampaign.org, helping out dying children in Africa and other third world countries? When I lived in the Midwest, I shoveled the walks of some neighborhood retirees in the winter, and I mowed their yards in the summer. There are tons of ways to glow by serving others. The thing Jesus said in Matthew 6:1-4 about meeting the needs of others was to not worry about who sees it. It is not about us; it's about letting the goodness be seen before the one doing good. We have the idea that we can only glow when we are present, but glowing is such a unique thing. Impact does not demand presence. When we demand attention for our good deeds, it dims our glow. Attention may be drawn, but not to the one who deserves it.

What can you start doing this week to meet the needs of some people around you?

free-flowing current

That's a good number of possible dimmer switches, and I'm sure there are many that are not mentioned above. What is a problem in my life may not be in yours. The most important thing to do is to be sensitive to and strengthen the weak areas of your glow. These are just switches for us to be aware of or avoid, so that we may glow the Light of Jesus to a dark world that needs His influence.

Let's jump back to the guys on the road to Emmaus; notice how their hearts were set ablaze.

> They said to each other, "Didn't our hearts burn within us as he talked with us on the road and explained the Scriptures to us? (NLT)

Their focus was correct. It's amazing how poorly we see and reflect when the focus is off. These two guys were focused on two things. First, they were focused on Scripture. We need to be students of the Word.

It's amazing how many glowing opportunities we can have after hearing from God daily. His Word becomes such a springboard of opportunity and a demonstration of being a light in the darkness. I recently challenged myself to read the whole Bible in 3 months (that's only 12 or 15 pages a day). It took me a little longer than 90 days, but it was amazing to see what being drenched in God's Word can do to your every day existence.

The other thing these two had going for them was that they were focused on Christ. To focus on any other goal or fix our gaze on any other object of devotion is to compromise where we glow, who we glow to, why we glow, the right moment to glow, and how bright we glow. Jesus, be the Center. It all hinges on our ability to spend time with Christ.

Ask yourself this question: does my heart burn within me? Is there a burning desire to let others see the light of Christ? Do you seem to be affected by these dimmer switches we just looked at? If you have room to grow in your glow, look again at the actions of these two guys on the Emmaus road.

> And within the hour they were on their way back to Jerusalem, There they found the eleven disciples and the others who has gathered with them, who said, 'The Lord has really risen! He appeared to Peter!'" (NLT)

Check out the courses of action they chose. First, they changed direction. Apparently, after truly experiencing Jesus, the current road being traveled is not good enough. When our focus changes so will our destination. If we are focused on the wrong thing, it's time for us to turn around. Focus on what's right. This is a decision no one can make for you.

Once you get turned around, the next thing we learn is to seek out other Christians. Not for isolation, but for community. It's been said that no man is an island. As much as we like our alone times, we need human interaction. And interaction with those who will encourage and direct our journey is invaluable. Find a church, or at least a small group, that you can plug into for accountability, encouragement, and instruction. And, unfortunately, for correction when it is needed.

Finally, these two guys were assured of His power. It all goes back to that supernatural power source. In all the "Omni's" of God (His omniscience, His omnipresence, His omnipotence), all I can be is Omni-nothing. We need to embrace the fact that without His power, we are just bulbs at the hardware store. We must be plugged into Him to be useful. We need His power to glow.

Six dimmer switches that diminish our glow are identified above. What are some other ones you can think of?

Illustration No. 4 The Glow-in-the-Dark Frisbee

we glow brighter when we spend time in the Son
chapter three

A few years ago, when I was living in Iowa, some friends of mine were getting ready for a vacation. They were on their way to California to visit some family. They planned to do the whole Mickey Mouse thing, hit some beaches and museums, and relax a whole lot by their uncle's pool. To prepare for this trip, they had to buy airline tickets and plan out some activities, which forced them to save up a humble amount of money for sites and souvenirs. They also had to make some arrangements with friends and family on the California end of things. One of my friends was also planning to hit the tanning booth ahead of time.

Now, tanning booths have never been my thing. When I do find the bronzing of my skin necessary, I prefer to get my UV rays from the sun itself and not some glowing incubator. But, when beaches and pools are in the near future, then I guess tans and swim suits must be considered. As opposed to getting a natural tan in sunny California, this one girl from Iowa opted for the fake bake.

We've all witnessed (i.e., gawked at) the fake bake gone badly, the curse of a tanning booth's ominous orange epidermis hue. Oh, those poor people! They try to make it all look natural, but come off looking like Scooter from the Muppets. Or an Oompa Loompa. The natural thing may take longer, but it usually lasts longer and looks better.

That leads to an interesting question which you may have never been asked, "How is your spiritual tan?" I know a lot of people who try to get the booth thing going with God. A little quick "shot o' God" here and there, and we hope it all turns out okay. Spiritually speaking, a "booth tan" is no substitute for direct Son-light. I've found that if we are to effectively glow, we need to spend time in God's light, just like a glow–in the-dark Frisbee, or whatever you like that glows in the dark (for my daughter, it was the stars on her ceiling). You can still use them without sunlight, but they were designed to glow. Just like us.

Why do you think we settle for fake-bake spirituality instead of getting the real thing?

I love the visual that Exodus 34:29-35 gives us:

> When Moses came down the mountain carrying the stone tablets inscribed with the terms of the covenant, he wasn't aware that his face glowed because he had spoken to the Lord face to face. And when Aaron and the people of Israel saw the radiance of Moses' face, they were afraid to come near him. But Moses called to them and asked Aaron and the community leaders to come over and talk with him. Then all the people came, and Moses gave them the instructions the Lord had given him on Mount Sinai. When Moses had finished speaking with them, he put a veil over his face. But whenever he went into the Tent of Meeting to speak with the Lord, he removed the veil until he came out again. Then he would give the people whatever instructions the Lord had given him, and the people would see his face aglow. Afterward he would put the veil on again until he returned to speak with the Lord." (NLT)

When Moses came down Mount Sinai carrying the two stone tablets inscribed with the terms of the covenant, he wasn't aware that his face had become radiant because he had spoken to the Lord. So when

we glow brighter when we spend time in the Son

Aaron and the people of Israel saw the radiance of Moses' face, they were afraid to come near him.

> But Moses called out to them and asked Aaron and all the leaders of the community to come over, and he talked with them. Then all the people of Israel approached him, and Moses gave them all the instructions the Lord had given him on Mount Sinai. When Moses finished speaking with them, he covered his face with a veil. But whenever he went into the Tent of Meeting to speak with the Lord, he would remove the veil until he came out again. Then he would give the people whatever instructions the Lord had given him, and the people of Israel would see the radiant glow of his face. So he would put the veil over his face until he returned to speak with the Lord. (NLT)

This was Moses' second trip up the mountain. The first time ended with the whole golden calf and smashed Ten Commandments thing. So here, Moses goes back to ask for another copy of the Ten Commandments and the 500th "second chance" for the people. God grants that 500th second chance and restores His covenant with Israel. That's the short historical version. But I love the part where it says Moses' face glowed. Not only that, but he also continued to glow so much that the children of Israel made him cover his face!

Do you have this kind of glow, or are you settling for some booth-tan that makes no impact on those around you? Do you glow with the glow brought on only by spending time in the Son-light? What does it take to glow like this?

the glow is a result of restoration

When you restore an old car, an antique, or an old house, it shines forth its newborn beauty. It may start out looking like a piece of junk, but a little "elbow-grease," as my grandpa called it, and it becomes new again. All the dings are repaired. Holes are filled. Rust removed. New paint is applied. Soon, the natural beauty of the original starts to appear. It happens with antiques of all sorts, and it can happen to you and me.

We may not think about this often, but God is in the refinishing business. In the last chapter of Revelation, Jesus says, "Behold! I make all things new again." When you spend quiet time with God (or loud time for that matter), let Him restore you while you are in His presence. Allow Him to strip away all the added baggage and crap, rub out all the scuffs and scratches, patch the holes, fix the brokenness, and re-finish you. This is what He wants to do. Philippians 1:6 tells us, "God will complete the work He started."

What is something in your life that has been started but not completed?

How will time in the Son help complete this restoration?

the glow is a result of vision

As incredible as being so close to God that it changes Moses' looks, the glow from his face wasn't the main thing Moses' would have talked about. During his second trip to the mountain, Moses actually saw God. Check it out. In Exodus 35:12-23, Moses got in the face of the Lord. "God, You keep telling me to take all these people to the Promised Land, but you never tell me who You're gonna send to help me out! Look, You talk to me by name. We're friends, right? You like me. If this is for real, let me see Your full intent so that I can see the big picture and get a better idea of what You're expecting me to do here. Remember, these are Your people I am leading, so You'd better treat them right!"

God responded, "Okay, how about if I go with you?! Just relax, Moses. Like, I'll have Bob Marley sing sometime thousands of years from now, 'every little thing is gonna be alright'."

Then Moses said the coolest thing. "Okay, but if You aren't going with us, we won't take another step. Because if You don't go with us, how will anyone ever know that we are Your people and You are our God? We'll just be like every other group of people on earth trying to figure it all out on their own."

And God replied to Moses, "Oh, I am good to my Word. I'll do what you asked for and more. And by the way, I am so proud of you, my friend."

Moses had one more request. Moses often had one more request. "God, I want to see You. Friends see each other, right? Lord, show me Your glory. Let me see your glow."

"My goodness is all around you, but I'll show you more," God answered. "I'll show my kindness and love and mercy to anyone I choose, but you can't see my face. Moses, you can't handle my glow! It's too much for you to take in, and it'd fry your brain! But stand in this little cut out part of this rock, I'll cover you with my hand until I pass, and then I'll lift my hand as I pass by. But there's no way you can look at my face."

Moses also saw all the promises and fullness of God's new covenant. On the mountain, laws were given. Expectations were reviewed. Plans for the Tabernacle, Ark of the Covenant, lamp stands, clothing for the priests, and everything else were spelled out for Moses to complete. In short, Moses received vision.

It's funny how staring at the sun hurts our vision, but looking upon the Son enhances our vision. Christ is all about restoring sight, physically and spiritually. We sing, "Open The Eyes Of My Heart," but do we really desire to see that way?

Think about this: What does God want to do with your life? It's an important question, because just a glimpse of this vision for your future gives you confidence and changes your demeanor. In other words, you glow! I've found that He may reveal only little bits of this vision at a time. But He has good reasons. This assures your return to His presence for step two. This assures that you'll depend on Him, not your ability. This assures that you won't screw it up by having too much knowledge. His presence gives us assurance.

I guess rhinoceroses can run faster than squirrels, like 30 miles per hour or something! That's a lot of weight moving that fast, heavier than my car. But the rhinos can only see about 30 feet ahead. This is just not safe! There's not a lot of vision behind that kind of movement. I think this is the same with my spiritual life. I don't need a lot of vision, just a glimpse, to move out for God. While I may prefer a 600-foot vision, God usually provides me with more like 30. Just a bit of vision from God and we glow.

Has God ever revealed Himself to you in some way?

Why would receiving insight from God affect the way we glow?

In Exodus, Moses comes down the mountain glowing, and the people notice. We, too, will glow and be noticed as a result of restoration and the assurance that vision gives us. Look at the impact Moses had after spending time with God. The first thing we notice is that the Tabernacle was finished (Exodus 40). Then, throughout the rest of Moses' life, we read vignettes that begin with "The Lord said to Moses …" Finally, the children of Israel were eventually delivered from the hands of the Egyptians. Deuteronomy 34:10-12 says this of Moses at the end of his life:

> There has never been another prophet in Israel like Moses, whom the Lord knew face to face. The Lord sent him to perform all the miraculous signs and wonders in the land of Egypt against Pharaoh, and all his servants, and his entire land. With mighty power, Moses performed terrifying acts in the sight of all Israel. (NLT)

That is a lot for one man to accomplish! And all of it was a result of capturing vision.

Speaking of vision, here's an interesting note: Deuteronomy 34:7 says that Moses lived to be 129 years old. His eyesight was clear, and he was strong as ever. Moses had been restored. He'd been given vision.

glow is a result of instruction

Mountaintop experiences like Moses' are associated with closeness to God and a readiness to receive His words. Probably my favorite mountaintop experience is found in Mark 9:2-10.

One day, Jesus asked Peter, James, and John to go on a little mountain hike. These three guys always got to do and see all the cool stuff! So they got up the mountain, and all of a sudden Jesus started looking a little different. His clothes "became dazzling white, far whiter than any earthly process could ever make them." The next thing you know, two dead guys showed up and started talking with Jesus. And not just any dead guys, but Moses and Elijah!

The three disciples didn't know what to say about this. Fear, wonder, and excitement have a way of stealing your words. But, as usual, Peter found something to say. "This is Awesome, Jesus! How about if I build a few tents: one for You, one for Moses, and one for

Elijah." In other words, "Let's just stay here." Then this big cloud came over them and a voice came out of it. Clouds weren't rare, but this one talked. The voice from the cloud said, "This Jesus is my beloved Son. Listen to and obey Him." Once their eyes jumped from the cloud back to Jesus, Moses and Elijah were gone. Only Jesus was with them.

How cool would it have been to be there?! I'm jealous. Peter, James, and John were regularly singled out to witness cool things like that. Think about the cloud coming over the mountain. This was called "Shekinah," God's presence, in the Old Testament. Then came the big voice from a cloud, "This is my Son, obey Him." Yep. As if Moses and Elijah weren't enough, God Himself showed up.

I really wish we knew more about this event. Like, how long were they up there? What were Jesus, Moses, and Elijah talking about? What happened after this? We do know that Peter went on to be a successful evangelist. And James wrote possibly the greatest book ever on Christian conduct. John was able to knock out a gospel, a few epistles, and a divine revelation of Heaven. One last question, "Did what they encountered at the Mount of Transfiguration impact this stuff?"

In the account in Mark, we are told that Moses and Elijah represented the law and the prophets. That's what all the commentaries and study Bibles tell us. Maybe their purpose was to teach a few confused disciples the validity of Jesus' ministry. Even following Jesus around for three years, I would've needed it. I think this a basic teaching that takes forever to sink in; that Jesus really is who He says He is.

I've found that in the presence of God there is always something for us to learn, about Him and about us. It has been my desire for many years now that when I spend time with God, I do not leave His presence without learning something new. Something I need. Please don't confuse instruction with information. We can gain a lot of information reading the genealogies in Scripture. But what instruction is there? Maybe that the Bible is the history of Jesus and that all of those people in the Old Testament were actually the forefathers of Jesus' earthly dad. Maybe that losers like us can still be a part of a grand plan, just like the liars, sluts, thieves and murderers that are a part of Jesus' lineage. I guess we move from information to instruction when the information is applied to our lives in a way that furthers the plan of God. Peter, James, and John had that experience on the Mount of Transfiguration.

we glow brighter when we spend time in the Son

Most of the time, we want to receive motivation or encouragement during our time with God. What can you do to be more open to receiving instruction from God?

the glow is a result of construction

Construction, yes; but not the kind Peter had ideas about. Not the three shacks for Moses, Elijah, and Jesus. The type of construction I'm talking about is much more important, and should last a lot longer. God's glory was seen up on that mountaintop, but it wasn't lived out until they came down the mountain into a valley. I'm the sort of guy who would be like Peter and want to stay up there. I always hated the last day of camps or retreats when we had to leave our communal life and get back to the real world. But as nice as a retreat is, staying there accomplishes little for the kingdom. The valleys of life need the light a whole lot more than the mountaintops.

Just a thought, but maybe mountaintops aren't meant to teach as much as they are meant to shape us. Surely Peter, James, and John were shaped by their experiences on the Mount of Transfiguration. In My Utmost for His Highest, Oswald Chambers writes, "We cannot stay on the Mount of Transfiguration, but we must obey the light we receive there, we must act it out."

Paul found this sort of inner transformation to be the most important thing in life. In writing to some Jesus-followers in Philippi, he encouraged them with these words:

> Whatever happens, my dear brothers and sisters, rejoice in the Lord. I never get tired of telling you these things, and I do it to safeguard your faith.
>
> Watch out for those dogs, those people who do evil, those mutilators who say you must be circumcised to be saved. For we who worship by the Spirit of God are the ones who are truly circumcised. We rely on what Christ Jesus has done for us. We put no confidence in human effort, though I could have confidence in my own effort if anyone could. Indeed, if others have reason for confidence in their own efforts, I have even more!
>
> I was circumcised when I was eight days old. I am a pure-blooded citizen of Israel and a member of the tribe of Benjamin—a real Hebrew if there ever was one! I was a member of the Pharisees, who demand the strictest obedience to the Jewish law. I was so zealous that I harshly persecuted the

church. And as for righteousness, I obeyed the law without fault.

I once thought these things were valuable, but now I consider them worthless because of what Christ has done. Yes, everything else is worthless when compared with the infinite value of knowing Christ Jesus my Lord. For his sake I have discarded everything else, counting it all as garbage, so that I could gain Christ and become one with him. I no longer count on my own righteousness through obeying the law; rather, I become righteous through faith in Christ. For God's way of making us right with himself depends on faith. I want to know Christ and experience the mighty power that raised him from the dead. I want to suffer with him, sharing in his death, so that one way or another I will experience the resurrection from the dead!

I don't mean to say that I have already achieved these things or that I have already reached perfection. But I press on to possess that perfection for which Christ Jesus first possessed me. No, dear brothers and sisters, I have not achieved it but I focus on this one thing: Forgetting the past and looking forward to what lies ahead, I press on to reach the end of the race and receive the heavenly prize for which God, through Christ Jesus, is calling us.
- Philippians 3:1-14 (NLT)

This is a serious construction! Our glow is a result of the construction that God desires to do in our lives. I am the clay; He is the potter. So many times while I am in His presence I have found God working this clay of a man into something useful. The thing is, clay can never be shaped into something of use and value until it is on the potter's wheel. Otherwise, it just remains a lump of clay. And so will we, unless we allow the presence of God to reconstruct and rebuild us into His image, an image that glows the Light of the World into the world.

Sometimes, God's blueprints for my life are not in accordance with the construction plans I have for the life I am trying to build. Why is it so challenging to let God shape our lives the way He sees fit?

the glow is a result of passion and zeal

There's one last way that our glow is strengthened from Son-light, and we learn it from Paul's encounter with Christ in Acts 9:1-22. Saul (Paul's name before Jesus got a hold of him) was bent on destroying Jesus-followers. Threats were as common for him as breathing. One day, Saul went to the high priest, the Jewish "top-dog," and asked for some help from the synagogues in Damascus in arresting all the Jesus-followers they could find. He wanted to get these Christians chained up and dragged back to Jerusalem for trial and death.

So, Saul went off to Damascus to kick some Jesus-follower butt. Before he got there, however, this big light shot down on him and made him lose his bearings so badly that he fell off his horse. He heard this voice saying, "Saul! Why are you being such a jerk to me?!" Saul responded, "Sir, I don't even know who you are!" "I'm Jesus," the voice says. "Remember? The one you are persecuting? Now get back up and go to Damascus, but don't do what you are planning to do. Instead, do what you are told to do."

The guys traveling with Saul were freaking out! They saw their friend get knocked off his horse and they heard the voice, but they couldn't see anyone doing or saying anything. Saul got up, but realized that he was blind. Leaving his white cane back in Jerusalem, Saul's friends led him by the hand to Damascus. He was blind for three days, and for those three days, Saul didn't eat or drink anything.

Here's how he got his sight back. There was this Jesus-follower in Damascus named Ananias. Jesus spoke to him at the same time as Saul. "Ananias! Go over to Straight Street to Judas' house. When you get there, ask for Saul of Tarsus. He's praying to me right now, so I know he's there. I showed him in a dream that a guy named Ananias would come over and lay hands on him and pray that he would be able to see again."

"You have to be kidding me, Jesus," Ananias said. "I've been reading about this guy in the paper! And I read just a few days ago that the leading priests in Jerusalem are sending him here to terrorize the Christians. He hates followers of You and does terrible things to them as often as he can. I follow You, so he's probably gonna do some bad things to me if I look for him! Are you sure about this?"

"Would you just do what I say," the Lord replied. "I have chosen to use Saul as my special tool to bring the Good News to the non-Jews and kings of other countries, as well as to other places in Israel. If you are worried about him being punished for all the bad stuff he's done, leave it in my hands. You just go and pray for him like I said."

So Ananias went and found Saul. He laid his hands on him and said, "Hey Saul. I'm kind of freaked out to be here. But the same Jesus who appeared before you on the road to Damascus sent me over to pray for you so that you can get you eyesight back and be filled with His Holy Spirit." All of the sudden, the scales dropped from Saul's eyes, and he could see again. Saul and Ananias went to the beach, and then Saul got baptized and hung out with the Jesus-followers in Damascus for a few days.

The next thing you know, Saul was in the synagogues telling them about Jesus and how He really is the Messiah. Everybody was amazed that this guy who hated Jesus-followers so badly was now a Jesus-follower himself. He came to arrest the followers of Jesus and instead he was preaching about Jesus and trying to get more people to follow The Way.

Saul kept right on preaching, and his sermons became more and more powerful. The Jews in Damascus couldn't argue with Saul's reasoning and proof that Jesus was indeed the Promised One, the Messiah.

Talk about having your world rocked!! It was true for both Paul and Ananias. The light of Christ is evident here. It's blinding! Singer/songwriter Andrew Peterson put it this way: Paul's blindness made him see. It's pretty awesome that even after He was murdered, Christ was still intent on restoring Saul's sight.

So what did Ananias think of all this? He was skeptical at least. His skepticism versus "Saul is my chosen instrument." Guess who won!

Now, I don't go to Home Depot just to collect things. I have no cherished relic of a wrench collection, nor do I want one. When I buy things from Home Depot, I want to use them. Christ is the same way. (Not in the Home Depot thing, but in the using what He's purchased part.) What Saul and Ananias experienced was a commissioning. Saul's experience was perfectly combined with service.

Is there a difference between a tool and an instrument? Do you think you are a tool or an instrument in God's hands?

Look again at verses 20-22: "And immediately he began preaching about Jesus in the synagogues, saying, 'He is indeed the Son of God!' All who heard him were amazed. 'Isn't this the same man who persecuted Jesus' followers with such devastation in Jerusalem?'

they asked. "And we understand that he came here to arrest them and take them in chains to the leading priests." Saul's preaching became more and more powerful, and the Jews in Damascus couldn't refute his proof that Jesus was indeed the Messiah.

Our time with God, in His presence, is not just for giggles. There is a charging element in these moments that are opportunities for God to encourage us to do something. Paul's glowing was so bright and so passionate that tact and protocol were sometimes afterthoughts (if they were even thought about at all). I only gain or regain that zeal, that passion, that kind of glow, by encountering Christ and spending time with Him.

Look at the results of spending time alone with God in intense communion: restoration, vision, instruction, construction, and passion. These are fuel sources for the fire. Ask yourself this question often, "What does God want to do in my life right now?"

You are holding this book in your hands. If you are really getting into this book, you are spending time in the indirect Son-light. Maybe you are being commissioned. The pages of this book are just the tanning booth; only Christ Himself is the Son. I'm glad you are reading this book, trust me. But please don't stop here! Make sure you spend time in His presence, not just in the presence of these words of mine.

Once you become sensitive to what God wants to do in your life, begin to determine what service Christ wants you to accomplish for Him. Start by looking at the stories we've read in this chapter: Moses led; Peter, James, and John taught and built the early church; and Paul converted and evangelized nations. So what's your purpose? How will you glow now that you've experienced time in the Son?

Illustration N⁰· 5 The Glow Worm

we glow brighter when we're under pressure
chapter four

I truly wish we didn't have to deal with this topic at all!! The fact is, that sometime today, we will head back down the mountain into the valley, and within minutes our "glow" will be challenged. Maybe its traffic or it could be our families. Money, or the lack of it, is also a culprit much of the time. At some time or another, it's probably been our job. Even the best relationships and most fulfilling blessings can challenge what God is working out in us. Regardless of where we live, we live under pressure. Stress. Temptation. Persecution. Pain. Our staying-power during these times speaks volumes to a world that needs the glow of the light within us. Sounds a lot like a Glow-Worm.

Remember these night-time buddies? Soft, little, cuddly, 12-inch stuffed green worms that, when you squeezed them, would glow a bit in the face, piercing the darkness to let you know all was well. A few more sophisticated models even sang a little tune to lull us back to sleep. Until the pressure was applied, it was just a stuffed animal. But with the squeeze came the glow. Pressure helped us realize its calming potential.

When was a time that you really felt like the pressure was on? What was the circumstance? Do/did you see God's hand in this situation at all?

How many times have I whined, ""But I'm too weak"; or "I'm tired"; or "I'm not strong enough to handle it all?!" Yeah, Randy. Exactly. Paul wrote in 2 Corinthians 4:7 that these perishable containers of bodies that we live in have a precious treasure in them; a treasure of light and power that glows inside of us. The purpose of something so magnificent being placed inside such a temporal being is so that the glory of what is seen can go to God and not us.

The point is, if we could handle it, people would only see us and not Christ in us. We need things to be difficult so that His glory can be seen in us. "I am weak but He is strong." The Bible calls us clay pots, jars of clay, earthen vessels, and perishable containers. All these things are fragile, temporary, easily overlooked and weak. Um, that sounds like us! But drop something of value into that jar and things change. Now, the jar hasn't changed, but what's in it has been magnified. Lord, may our lives do that in our weakest, most vulnerable times.

I've discovered that a few things have to happen in order for us to glow when the pressure is on.

perseverance helps us glow

When we maintain our spiritual composure through the hard times, people notice. In the early 90s, I worked at a diner in Des Moines. On Sunday November 29, 1992, two friends of mine were murdered while working there. Cara was at the register, and Tim was decorating the Christmas tree. The restaurant was buzzing with activity. Burgers were being fried, beers were being poured, salads were being made, and malts were being served. Then a young man walked in the door and stuck a gun in the back of my friend, Cara's, head. She thought someone was joking around and turned to see what was going on. A trigger was pulled, and Cara fell to the floor. Tim came running to help, and the gunman popped him in the forehead. Then the shooter took the money from the register and left everyone with the mess he created. Two vibrant lives, with futures of opportunity ahead, were taken for a gang initiation, resulting in two murders and a few hundred bucks.

I'd dealt with death before. My grandparents had passed away, along with a few elderly friends in my church and a handful of friends from high school and college. But it was different this time. This time, life was intentionally taken. It made no sense and the pain was deep in all the friends and family at the diner. We all met with grief and tragedy counselors for a couple weeks. Many had the visual of the whole encounter etched into their heads.

We were all looking for help to move on, despite the losses we had experienced. Some tried stepping up their drinking and other chemical habits. Others sunk into clinical depression. Some lost themselves in the business of sexual pursuits. One person simply took off, and I haven't seen or heard from her since. Still others sought solace in hobbies to get their minds off the incident. I turned to God. What I experienced was a peace that I couldn't explain. The pressure was felt. The pain was real, gnawing, and deep. But so was the comfort of God. The evidence of the impact God was having on me during this tough time was displayed in one question that was repeatedly asked of me by my fellow employees. "Randy, how are you dealing with all of this so well?" This was a tough time in my life; easily in the top three "suckiest" things to happen in my life. And being a Christian, eyes were on me to see how I'd handle it. It was an unfortunate opportunity to glow.

Isaiah wrote in chapter 43, verses 1-3:

> But now, O Jacob, listen to the Lord who created you. O Israel, the one who formed you says, "Do not be afraid, for I have ransomed you. I have called you by name; you are mine. When you go through deep waters, I will be with you. When you go through rivers of difficulty, you will not drown. When you walk through the fire of oppression, you will not be burned up; the flames will not consume you. For I am the Lord, your God, the Holy One of Israel, your Savior... (NLT)

God said "I'll be there." And I really wish He'd said, "I'll get you out of it." But how could He be glorified if

I never faced problems? If this were the case, I wouldn't even need Him. No matter how hard you try to avoid them, trouble, difficulty, and oppression will happen. The Bible calls them "waters," "rivers," "fire," and "flame." Get this: what happens when they happen determines what happens.

The point I'm trying to make is this: stick it out! Persevere. Know that if we bear His name, if His image is stamped on us, He'll never bring us anything that will bring Him eternal shame. We are told in 2 Corinthians 4:8-10

> We are pressed on every side by troubles, but we are not crushed. We are perplexed, but not driven to despair. We are hunted down, but never abandoned by God. We get knocked down, but we are not destroyed. Through suffering, our bodies continually share in the death of Jesus so that the life of Jesus may also be seen in our bodies. (NLT)

Here's another verse that I wish God had left out of The Book. But He didn't. I'd rather not have to face suffering, getting crushed, broken, perplexed, hunted, or knocked down. As we persevere, instead of being crushed by life's blows, we'll grow stronger. Sticking through the tough times brightens our glow.

Paul goes on in 2 Corinthians 6:4-10:

> In everything we do, we show that we are true ministers of God. We patiently endure troubles and hardships and calamities of every kind. We have been beaten, been put in prison, faced angry mobs, worked to exhaustion, endured sleepless nights, and gone without food. We prove ourselves by our purity, our understanding, our patience, our kindness, by the Holy Spirit within us, and by our sincere love. We faithfully preach the truth. God's power is working in us. We use the weapons of righteousness in the right hand for attack and the left hand for defense. We serve God whether people honor us or despise us, whether they slander us or praise us. We are honest, but they call us impostors. We are ignored, even though we are well known. We live close to death, but we are still alive. We have been beaten, but we have not been killed. Our hearts ache, but we always have joy. We are poor, but we give spiritual riches to others. We own nothing, and yet we have everything. (NLT)

Further, in 2 Corinthians 12:6-10, he writes:

> ...I don't want anyone to give me credit beyond what they can see in my life or hear in my message, even though I have received such wonderful revelations from God. So to keep me from becoming proud, I was given a thorn in my flesh, a messenger from Satan to torment me and keep me from becoming proud.
>
> Three different times I begged the Lord to take it away. Each time he said, "My grace is all you need. My power works best in weakness." So now I am glad to boast about my weaknesses, so that the power of Christ can work through me. That's

we glow brighter when we're under pressure

> why I take pleasure in my weaknesses and in the insults, hardships, persecutions, and troubles that I suffer for Christ. For when I am weak, then I am strong. (NLT)

Do you think maybe Paul knew what he was talking about here? Only with the Holy Spirit working in us can we withstand this temptation to quit. Left to our own inclinations, strength, and abilities, we all are much more likely to give up rather than persevere. But that's why God gives us His Holy Spirit. With His help, we can struggle and fight our way through the things that bind us, and experience the new life awaiting us. A butterfly has to struggle and fight its way out of a cocoon, and, if it doesn't, it will never develop. I'd like to help it out. But if I did, I'd seal its doom. Through the struggle comes the strength to fly.

Similarly, the beauty of a diamond is only seen after the pressure is put on the coal. Through the pressure comes beauty and power. Or, take a rug for instance: in order to lose the wrinkles, it has to be flattened out and walked on.

Wow! How much strength, beauty, power, or straightening have I robbed myself of by taking the easy way out or asking to be rescued from what was meant to shape me?! Stick it out. Don't give up. Persevere. Glow.

Reflect back on that situation you wrote about earlier. Did you have any sense of God's presence during that time of "deep waters and great trouble?" You are here now, so how did you make it through the difficulty?

making the most of it helps us glow

Whether you like it or not, your attitude is showing people what you're made of. If you are anything like me, this is a quick bucket of water on an external glow. My attitude sucks from time to time. I remember growing up, and my mom always saying, "You watch your attitude, boy!" I've never outgrown the need for this admonishment.

2 Peter 1:5-8 tells us to:

> Make every effort to respond to God's promises. Supplement your faith with a generous provision

> of moral excellence, and moral excellence with knowledge, and knowledge with self-control, and self-control with patient endurance, and patient endurance with godliness, and godliness with brotherly affection, and brotherly affection with love for everyone.
>
> The more you grow like this, the more productive and useful you will be in your knowledge of our Lord Jesus Christ. (NLT)

Think about this: the whole purpose of persevering and enduring all the stuff we have to face is to move us into godliness. Everything you just read about perseverance shows us that there are better things ahead. This too shall pass. I think I heard a cliché about this. Something about when the world gives you lemons…

Now, it's hard for me to look at pressure as a gift from God, but it is. My job is to find out what's in it for me! When you can't seem to take it anymore, rejoice, knowing that God thinks you're stronger than you thought you were. I like to fall asleep and wake up to music. During the most trying time of my life, I woke up one morning to a worship song by Tim Hughes called "He's Got the Whole World in His Hands." No, it's not the song we all learned as little kids, but it does share the same sentiment. I remember lying in my bed thinking, "God, I know you say we won't have to go through anything we can't endure.

But, God, just how strong do you think I am? I can't handle this!" Sometimes it's the simple fact of God's promise, and not my understanding of how it works, that helps us make the most of it. And He promises to never let us face anything we can't handle. Plus, He equips us with new mercies every morning just to deal with each new day's pressures! We can almost always learn something from life's strife.

I'm not saying you should pitch a tent and throw a party. I am to rejoice in my sufferings, not about them. I am saying that the way we look at the crap of life is a determining factor in how well Christ is reflected around us.

A few nuggets from the Scriptures include: "Don't worry, pray about everything," and "In all things give thanks." You see, there are two things that put us in the company of God, prayer and praise. From there, we can see our situation from a new perspective. It's funny how small our "big problems" look from His viewpoint. In addition, as we have already seen, His presence strengthens our glow on its own.

I love this story in 2 Kings. The prophet Elisha is under attack. His foes are hunting him down to take him out. One morning, his servant gets up for some coffee and Fruit Loops, and looks out the kitchen window. What he sees are battalions stationed around them preparing for attack. "Dude! We are going down!" the servant cries to Elisha. But Elisha tells him to look again. "Seriously?" the servant replies. "Look again? I know what I saw, man." When he looks out the window this time, he sees angel armies outnumbering their foes. The impending battle didn't even occur. The battle was fought in the heavens, and Elisha and his servant didn't have to get their hands dirty at all.

When was a time where your attitude about something changed when you saw it from a different perspective?

finishing strong helps us glow

My brother and I used to play basketball a lot growing up. It was a blast for me when I was in high school and he was in junior high. I could totally dominate him, on the court and off. But when he hit high school, Perry grew a lot. I am about 5 feet 10 inches tall. My brother is about 6 feet 3 inches. I can talk about how he's gonna get pummeled on the court. I can tell him I'll block the shots he takes. I can prepare him to go down.

I learned a lot from these experiences after my brother got older and taller. One was to learn to focus on my outside shot. If I drove to the hoop, his 5-inch height advantage would result in blocked shots. If I missed my outside shot, there's no way I'd outrebound him. Another thing I learned is that nothing looks dumber than some guy talking trash and losing in the end; on the court or in the faith. I can tout how great my walk is and proclaim Christ until I'm blue in the face; but if I'm not able to run the course and finish the race, it doesn't amount to much. The glow is unimportant if it doesn't last to the end.

Acts 7:54-60 is the best biblical example of finishing strong:

> The Jewish leaders were infuriated by Stephen's accusation, and they shook their fists at him in rage. But Stephen, full of the Holy Spirit, gazed steadily into heaven and saw the glory of God, and he saw Jesus standing in the place of honor at

> God's right hand. And he told them, "Look, I see the heavens opened and the Son of Man standing in the place of honor at God's right hand!"
>
> Then they put their hands over their ears and began shouting. They rushed at him and dragged him out of the city and began to stone him. His accusers took off their coats and laid them at the feet of a young man named Saul.
>
> As they stoned him, Stephen prayed, "Lord Jesus, receive my spirit." He fell to his knees, shouting, "Lord, don't charge them with this sin!" And with that, he died. (NLT)

I hope I never have to face what Stephen did. I pray I'll never have to deal with the pressures of boulders being thrown at me. And I can only hope that I have the spiritual stamina to finish my time on earth so boldly. I pray I can face any struggles I encounter with the same amount of character. How are you finishing your time of persecution and pressure? The words "forgive them Lord" spoken by Stephen. That spoke volumes. There's no way for us to know, but maybe it was here that the Holy Spirit started dealing with Paul/Saul. The way Stephen finished created a whole new beginning for Paul/Saul. You never know what impact you'll have by just finishing well.

· · · · ·

Jesus was a terrible marketing/sales manager, but a great Savior/minister. He was always saying things like, "If you follow Me, you're going to get messed with ... I promise." Really? That's not a promise of God that I want! He even assured us that when we're under pressure, it's probably because we're glorifying Him. Either that or He's refining us and making us brighter reflectors. Nonetheless, the fact is that we will be pressed. But persevere; make the most of it, and finish strong.

Take some time and look at the life of Joseph in Genesis 37-50. How is his life a biblical example of glowing brighter when the pressure is on?

Illustration No. 6 The Glow Stick

we glow brighter when we're broken
chapter five

The Christian life would be a lot easier if the Bible hadn't given us the benchmark of "I must decrease that He might increase." There are so many things that are easy for us to "amen" to but rather difficult to flesh out. I think this one may be harder because it involves so much flesh. We're talking about pride here. ("I'm better at controlling my pride than you are.") God's Word tells us, or maybe promises us, "pride comes before a fall." One of the best statements about pride came from a California preacher named Ralph Torres. At a conference in Ft. Worth, I heard him say, "God's not out to hurt your pride; He's out to kill it!"

In the last chapter, we talked about how we glow brighter when the pressure is on. Sometimes the pressure just keeps growing until we get to a point of brokenness. Now, there are a few ways you can be broken. You can have no money. I've been broke that way. Laws can be broken. Unfortunately, I've broken a few of those as well. And a horse can be broken, too. But the broken we're going to look at is like when a vase or a plate is cracked or shattered. I haven't been broken like this too badly, other than a broken nose, toes, and a couple of ribs. And most of those include a story about my brother. Remember, Paul said that he felt the pressure, but he wasn't broken. This leads to another way we can be broken. In Psalm 51, there is something about "a broken spirit and a contrite heart." And I have definitely been there a few times.

In the times I have been truly broken, I have discovered that a joy, comfort and completeness followed. Not right away, mind you; but it came. During one of my biggest times of brokenness, my friend Michael saw hope long before I did. His words to me were simple and profound: "Randy, you can't drink grapes." For a good wine to come out of grapes, they have to be crushed and broken. Transformed. They have to die to life on the vine so that they can bring life to a meal, in glasses shared by friends and family.

Throughout Scripture, God refers to Himself and His desire to be called "I AM." I've found only one name to truly be great: the name of Jesus. In the gospels, He said, "I AM the way, I AM the truth, I AM the life …" If He is I AM, that leaves one name for us: I Am Not. In our living of the Christian life, we will either attract or distract people from Jesus. Pride is the biggest distraction we offer. This is why the Bible says "I must decrease, that He may increase." What are you doing to amplify and increase His name? God, just break us wide open, and let You run out. I've found that when I am broken, I glow more. It's a lot like a glow stick.

These little plastic tubes of mystery liquid do little good unless they are bent and broken. They are interesting and jovial just as they are, but when they are broken their true purpose shines by, well … shining. That one little stick can light the path for a lost hiker, draw attention to someone stranded by the road, or be a warning that something is ahead. One little broken glow stick has this potential and so much more. And so do we, when we break ourselves and begin to glow.

One woman that followed Jesus did a great job of exemplifying this death to pride. Let's look at what she did; what motivated her, and the significance of her action. Her story is quickly told in Luke 7:36-38:

> One of the Pharisees asked Jesus to have dinner with him, so Jesus went to his home and sat down to eat. When a certain immoral woman from that city heard he was eating there, she brought a beautiful alabaster jar filled with expensive perfume. Then she knelt behind him at his feet, weeping. Her tears fell on his feet, and she wiped them off with her hair. Then she kept kissing his feet and putting perfume on them. (NLT)

A little more detail is given in Mark 14:1-9:

> It was now two days before Passover and the Festival of Unleavened Bread. The leading priests and the teachers of religious law were still looking for an opportunity to capture Jesus secretly and kill him. "But not during the Passover celebration," they agreed, "or the people may riot."
>
> Meanwhile, Jesus was in Bethany at the home of Simon, a man who had previously had leprosy. While he was eating, a woman came in with a beautiful alabaster jar of expensive perfume made from essence of nard. She broke open the jar and poured the perfume over his head.
>
> Some of those at the table were indignant. "Why waste such expensive perfume?" they asked. "It could have been sold for a year's wages and the money given to the poor!" So they scolded her harshly.
>
> But Jesus replied, "Leave her alone. Why criticize her for doing such a good thing to me? You will always have the poor among you, and you can help them whenever you want to. But you will not

> always have me. She has done what she could and has anointed my body for burial ahead of time. I tell you the truth, wherever the Good News is preached throughout the world, this woman's deed will be remembered and discussed." (NLT)

Now, some say the woman mentioned in the account from Luke was Mary Magdalene, and the woman in the account from Mark was Mary the sister of Martha and Lazarus. Still others say it was two different women, not even named Mary. I think these scriptures refer to both Mary's in individual acts of devotion, but what do I know? What I do know is that what she did has been, and will be, talked about for years. That's a serious glow.

I've had a time of brokenness, where I was laid out at the feet of Jesus. As we look deeper at this story from the Gospels, let me share a bit of my story, and illustrate how brokenness helped increase my glow. I pray that your moments of brokenness can lead to similar opportunities to let Jesus be seen in your response to life's painful circumstances.

What did she do? . . .

she poured out oil

This woman held an alabaster jar/box containing expensive perfume. It was a precious stone piece containing the best for the Very Best. Since women of the day were not employed, this was her most valuable possession. Historians tell us that, at that time in the Middle East, this jar of nard was more than likely going to be used as a marriage dowry sometime in the future. Yet, Mary chose to lay it all aside for the anointing of her Lord.

When I read this story, I don't picture her gently breaking a little hole in the top and then shaking it out like some Tabasco sauce bottle. She didn't just shake some out the spout; I think she broke the neck and dumped it all out! It was like she was saying, "Nothing for me. It's all for you." That jar was empty by the time she finished with it. All her future plans, hopes, and dreams of finding and securing a man were emptied out on THE Man.

What do you hold as most valuable? Do you find your identity wrapped up in that? What could be wrong with your identity being tied to what you hold precious?

One day, I came home from a pastor's trip in Iowa, and when I went to give my wife a hug, I was told that she "couldn't do this anymore." And by "this" she meant the whole marriage thing. A few days later, I found out that she was in love with another man. This was the woman I chose to marry, the one whom my daughter called "mommy." I was the assistant pastor in my church, was heard all over on the Christian radio station in town, and was a very visible Christian man in my community. This wasn't how things are supposed to work out. I valued my family, and now it was being ripped apart, not just by some tension. This Christian couple had a third person added into the equation. And it was shattering my family, my image, and my ministry.

she washed His feet with her tears

She had tears. I'm not too smart, but I think this implies that Mary was crying at Jesus' feet. Not just a little whimpering. This chick was crying enough to move the dust off His feet.

If this really was Mary of Bethany, this was not the first time she had spent time at His feet. Remember the story of when Jesus was in Bethany with Martha and Mary? Martha was busy in the kitchen, and Mary was content just to hang with Jesus. It's the conflict of simply being with Jesus versus doing stuff for Jesus. Nonetheless, this woman found her place of honor at the feet of the Honored.

When has a crisis driven you to the feet of Jesus?

During that pastor's conference, Jack Hayford said that nothing drives us to the Father in prayer like a good crisis. Little did I know that those words were a foreshadowing of the days and weeks to come. My wife didn't want marriage counseling. The marriage was over. Her heart was with another man. What was I supposed to do to save my marriage? It was beyond my control. All I could do was to regularly ask God to fix it, to fix me, to comfort me and strengthen me as I was facing this crisis. These were not light prayers, but a heavy yearning. I was seeing the broken spirit and contrite heart thing in a whole new light.

Mary didn't just soak Jesus' sneakers; she dried His feet with her hair. Can you hear Jesus? "Anybody got a towel? Simon?! My sandals are soggy now." That wasn't Jesus' response. There was no need for that response, really. Mary put her hair in her hand, and rubbed it on His feet.

I'm a bald man (by choice). But at one time I had huge "Flock-of-Seagulls" hair. It was one massive hybrid new-wave mullet that was brought to life each morning with mouse, gel, hairspray, and more mouse. I know what long, dirty hair feels like. Realistically, how clean and fresh could Mary's hair have been after this? Women (and some guys I know) take pride in how kempt they are. This kind of activity would have made Mary look rather tattered.

I used to take a lot of pride in my image. People knew me around town. Rarely did my wife and I go somewhere where we didn't run into someone I knew or someone who knew me. When we would go out to eat, waiters would recognize my voice from the radio. And now I was unkempt. I didn't want to go anywhere where people would notice me. My demeanor was different. My joy was robbed. And the happy Christian family I thought I had was now seen for what it was. A fraud.

What do you take pride in? What would it look like to offer this to Jesus?

then she kisses His feet

So, does anyone want to smooch my soles? First it was her perfume on His feet, then her tears, followed by her hair. To cap it all off, now her lips were placed on Jesus' feet. Clean feet or not, that's kind of sick! Kissing the feet of someone is the position of a slave (or maybe worse) and not a friend's place! But it was the service Mary deemed necessary.

The Psalmist uses the phrase, "Kiss the Son." This is not about making out with Jesus. This is about worship and honor. The hardest thing to do in our lowest moments is to worship Jesus. To be the lone worshipper in a room full of gawkers is not the first thing that occurs to many of us.

Why is worshipping God so difficult during a crisis?

Do we think less of God during these times, or do we simply think of worshipping Him less often?

In the previous chapter, I told a story about waking up to the worship song "He's Got the Whole World in His Hands." That story occurred during this time of my life. Worship wasn't my natural reaction, but I did find it valuable and important to offer praise during my storm. Not FOR my storm, but IN my storm. I tell you, with my prayer life amped up, my time reading the Bible amped up, and my worship habits now being challenged, I was spending a ton of time in the Son. And as we observed dozens of pages ago, we glow brighter when we spend time in the Son. So, What motivated her to do this?

brokenness

The first and most important thing we must recognize about Mary's actions is that they were birthed out of brokenness. Jesus was at Simon's house. Simon's family was there, along with a few friends, maybe even the mayor! Jesus and His disciples were there. All of these people sitting around getting ready to eat dinner. And all of a sudden this woman with a reputation comes barging in the door uninvited, unaccepted, and uninhibited. Then, in front of everyone, Mary does all this perfume-tears-hair-lips stuff. She didn't walk in and ask, "Um, Jesus, can we go someplace alone for a few minutes?" NO! Mary realizes who she's not, in light of Who He is, and her reaction culminates in the "I AM versus I AM NOT."

How have you demonstrated your humility before God?

Mary's inner brokenness demanded a physical response. Jesus had, at some point, touched her life in a way she could no longer ignore. She laid all decorum, public opinion, and social norms aside and barged into a stranger's house so she could minister to the One who had ministered to her in such a powerful way. Brokenness of spirit led to brokenness of all that was important in her life.

For me, it was a brokenness of what was important in my life that led to my broken spirit. I remember when I had to come clean about the reality that my marriage was ending. I stood in front of my church, stared at the floor, cried in front of them all, and told them that I was facing a divorce. I was a leader to these people. If I couldn't do it, how could I really lead? How could I encourage others when I was struggling to find encouragement myself? I was humiliated. I was weak, broken, confused, and worried. I was at the end of my rope, and I was asking people to help me hold on.

safe environment

I think Mary was aware of a certain safety in the presence of Jesus. It wasn't just a confidence that arose when she walked into Simon's home and saw Jesus, but a confidence that had been growing in her as she watched how Jesus interacted with others. Mary was confident of this safety even before she went to Simon's house. Even with all these people gawking, pointing fingers, and whispering about her self-sacrifice, she knew she was perfectly safe doing so in Christ's presence. He'd proven this to her time and again, like in Bethany with Martha. ("Martha! Leave Mary alone! She's found a right place to be.") Christ understood why she was doing what she was doing.

According to Mark 14:6-8, Jesus replied:

> But Jesus replied, "Leave her alone. Why criticize her for doing such a good thing to me? You will always have the poor among you, and you can

help them whenever you want to. But you will not always have me. She has done what she could and has anointed my body for burial ahead of time. (NLT)

Do you find safety in the presence of Jesus? Why?

What was remarkable about coming clean about my broken marriage was how much acceptance and help I found. Now, I know that others who may read this and have faced divorce have not found this in their churches or from their spiritual leaders. Let me say right off that I am so sorry that Jesus was represented to you this way. When Jesus said "Come to me all who are weary and heavy laden," he didn't finish the sentence with "unless you have been divorced."

During my divorce, I saw a counselor. We didn't talk about fixing my marriage or fixing my wife. We talked about fixing and strengthening me. In one of those sessions, we were looking at my fears, and I found the safety, comfort and tenderness of the Savior like I never had before. It's amazing how much security we can find when we quit trying to save ourselves.

this was an act of passion and intimacy

You don't just go up to strangers and do what Mary did. You can try, though. Go down to the bus station with some Calvin Klein Obsession and ask a traveler to take off their shoes so you can make 'em smell better. Just try it. You'd get so beat up! And you don't do this just for kicks and giggles. Nothing better to do today, so why not anoint some poor old chap's smelly old feet?!

I think you'd only do this for someone you care about deeply; perhaps family or a close friend. This was Mary's heart; she cared very much for her teacher-friend Jesus Christ. She'd listened to all of His sermons, watched Him heal, and had dinner with Him. They were not just acquaintances; they knew and loved each other like friends do. Mary was willing to put her private feelings on public display.

How do you show passion and intimacy?

While I was at that pastor's conference, I was asked to speak at a men's retreat. I agreed, and I had even worked out an initial outline of what I was going to share. It was months away when I said yes. Little did I know how far removed I'd be from the circumstances under which I accepted the invitation. I'd forgotten about my commitment, when Tom called and asked how everything was going. I told him how it was going. Crappy. My family was falling apart. My marriage was over. I was feeling worthless and like I had failed so many people by being in an imperfect marriage. And how, in spite of all of this, I was feeling closer to God than I ever had before.

Tom demonstrated unconditional love and acceptance to me at this time. When Tom explained to me that he'd had asked Randy the person to speak, not Randy's circumstances, I began to see a Jesus who manages to separate a person from his failures. Tom said that we are all shaped by the things that happen to us, but we are not defined by them. Then he told me that he still wanted me to speak to the men. My act of passion and intimacy was to stand in front of a hundred guys and talk to them. To tell them about how where we are in life is only part of a bigger story of adventure, even though it's easy to think that this is the whole thing right here and right now. I stood before these guys and talked candidly about how I was feeling, the good the bad and the ugly. I cried as I talked about the love of God, the grace of God, and the redemption of God. I cried as I told them that sometimes our stories aren't all wrapped up and fixed like we want. And I cried when I encouraged them to finish their part of God's story with boldness and honor. The passion I have for Jesus, and the intimacy we share, was clearly seen by the men at that Iowa campground.

this was an act of humility

From the "here's my perfume" offering to crying hard in front of friends and strangers; from rubbing her beautiful hair on a guy's feet to kissing those feet … How selfless can you get? Not just in looking at Mary's actions, but really think about this. How selfless can you get?

I'll be honest, my pride needed to be knocked down a bit. I took a lot of things for granted. I had some misplaced priorities. I was into the perception of reality far more than the reality itself. I needed to be humbled. I do not believe that God destroyed my marriage so that I could learn a lesson in humility. But I did learn a very valuable one.

The thing is, we will all be humbled. The Bible says that "Every knee will bow and every tongue confess that Jesus Christ is Lord." We will all bow before God some day. I have come to believe that bowing before God can happen three ways. First, we can choose to be humble. This is the easiest way to be humbled and the most difficult. Second, we can be humbled by circumstances. Divorce, layoffs, terminal illnesses, foreclosures, or deaths can provide valuable lessons in humility. Finally, one day, God will humble all those not already humbled. I have decided that I'd rather put my knee to the dirt and bow before Him than have Him drive my knee into the dirt.

What lessons have you learned about humility?

When have you seen humility demonstrated?

"I must decrease so that He can increase." That's what Paul said. This woman decided to decrease on her own, and it was such a humble demonstration that Jesus said we'd be talking about it forever. And two thousand years later we are.

What was the significance of Mary's actions? ...

a sacrifice is giving something of worth

I have a lot of CDs. More than I can count, honestly. Sometimes I don't even know what I have loaned to people. I give a lot of my CDs away. Although the ones receiving them may find value in my gifts, they really aren't putting me out. I'm not sacrificing anything. Why? Because it's not a sacrifice if you don't sacrifice something. Giving away a spare CD in my vast abundance is not sacrificing much. But Mary's perfume was expensive; it was worth something to her. She valued it. So did one of the disciples, claiming the perfume could have been sold instead, and shouldn't have been wasted on the Messiah's feet.

What do you value most? Are you willing to lay it down at His feet?

As I struggled through my divorce, I laid my pride and reputation down at Jesus' feet. And honestly, they were pretty beaten up when I gave them to Him. I couldn't do anything with them, so I offered them to Jesus. And He redeemed it. That's what He does. He is all about taking our sacrifices and making something new out of them.

My marriage was never repaired. I spent a couple years as a single dad. Then my daughter picked out the woman she wanted to be her new mom and my new wife. I have a whole new life now. Marriage has been redeemed for me. And one of the things I have learned about making my family life more vibrant is to regularly sacrifice my pride and my reputation. I am very serious about my commitments, but I do not take myself too seriously as I keep them.

her tears signified remorse

The closer we get to Christ, the more we realize how unlike Him we are. It's odd when you think about it, isn't it? We are challenged to draw closer to Christ so we can become more like Him. Yet, when we do draw close, the first thing we realize is how far we are missing the mark. I find this so frustrating! It about makes you want to cry, right? Exactly! When was the last time your spiritual shortcomings actually caused you remorse? David wrote that "a broken spirit and a contrite heart are more desirable to God than offerings." This act of Mary's sure must've pleased Him.

Are tears a sign of weakness? Why do people think so?

I am no longer ashamed to cry. I cry at films, I cry during worship, and I cry when I talk about how much I love my family. And I really don't care who is around. I was on a business trip with a room full of marketing peeps. We were talking about a product that really emphasized the inner beauty of little girls, and I started to cry as I talked about how important that message is for young girls. How I want my daughter to fully realize how beautiful she already is in my eyes and in her Heavenly Father's eyes. I was missing my daughter that day, I guess. Once humility is gone, it's a lot easier to be honest with our feelings. I grew up hearing "walk it off" every time I was hurt. One time, my mom broke her foot, and my dad told her to walk it off. Seriously. (For the record, dad didn't know that mom had broken her foot.)

I don't always walk it off. Sometimes, we can't walk off the pain we feel. We can't walk off the fact that we are pros at sinning. It may be that we are too embarrassed to admit what we did. Or that the crap we are facing is just too much of a burden to carry. We can't always walk it off. Sometimes we need to cry it off.

her service to Christ signified honor

When we look at everything that Mary did for Jesus, all those acts were performed to show great respect. Here's a house full of people (political, religious, and financial leaders), but only One Who was honorable. Only One worth the honoring. Honor and passion can go hand in hand. You rarely honor someone in a whimsical way; if so, honor may not have been shown.

I wonder if Mary thought this out. Did she plan it? Or maybe she was so overwhelmed with Christ that she couldn't help but dump oil, cry out, scrub His feet with her locks, and kiss Him. To honor becomes an act of worship.

You know what? I am a divorcee. I have been hurt deeply by the actions of others. The best way for me to honor God during this was to take Jesus words about forgiving seriously. My daughter has never heard me say bad things about her mom or her relationship. Never. I do not hate my ex-wife. I take the high road, make sacrifices, and ask forgiveness when I am wrong in my dealings with my ex. It's not because it's second nature for me, or because I am a holy person. I do it because I want to honor the One who redeemed me, my marriage, and my reputation.

A thought on worshipping God: worship should always honor God and humble you. Anything less, any self exaltation or diversion of the attention He deserves, any lifting up of man or man-made institutions or things, means worship is not taking place. I find it's easy to say I have passion for Christ. But am I honoring Him by throwing myself at His feet with no regard to what it's costing me; without concern of money; without concern of pride; without concern of time?

How do you worship God? How do you prepare yourself to worship Him?

she was driven by gratitude

Imagine that a big banquet is being thrown for you. People come, give their regards, and present you with an award for all your goodness. After we've been honored, we usually offer our thanks. This was not so with Mary and Jesus. Here, she did the honoring and the thanking. "Oh thank you …". Smooch-smooch on His feet. "It's my privilege to serve you. Thanks for allowing me!" We don't hear that too often!

The gratitude from Mary is for Jesus' response to all this. Jesus pretty much tells everyone at the house (not His house, mind you), "Get off her back! She's doing a great thing here!" Jesus understood her so well that He just let her do her thing. He could have responded a thousand ways; but only one was seen, compassion mixed with empathy. That's something to be thankful for.

What is it about God that you are most thankful for?

. . . . .

Brokenness like Mary's demands a response. Jesus said, "People are going to talk about this for a long time." That makes me think. Are people talking about my brokenness? Not in an arrogant way, but I want my brokenness to be the talk of the town so that the glory of God may be seen through my actions. Have I been so broken that Christ is shining through this clay pot of my life? 2 Corinthians 4:7 says:

> We now have this light shining in our hearts, but we ourselves are like fragile clay jars containing this great treasure. This makes it clear that our great power is from God, not from ourselves. (NLT)

I know a guy named Ned who went through a very bitter divorce a few years before I did. Ned doesn't follow the Jesus way. As we were talking one day, Ned started demeaning his ex-wife, my ex-wife, and the general idea of marriage. I totally understood why

Ned was saying those things, but I didn't agree with him at all. So I stopped him. He mentioned that he never heard me talk bad about my ex-wife, the institution of marriage, or any of that sort of thing. Then he said, "Is it because of Jesus that you don't do this?" I had a great opportunity to tell Ned that it wasn't because I was afraid of making Jesus mad, but simply that Jesus gave me a new way of looking at it all. "I wish I could see it that way," Ned said. I responded, "Ned, let me tell you how you can …"

Mary was broken, but the result of her actions turned all eyes on Christ. Our brokenness should do the same. Are you willing to be that broken? Are you willing to throw your life at His feet, not caring about who sees? And while we are there, are you willing to see the warm glow in His eyes, and then, through humility, refract that warmth to a world that is cold to His touch?

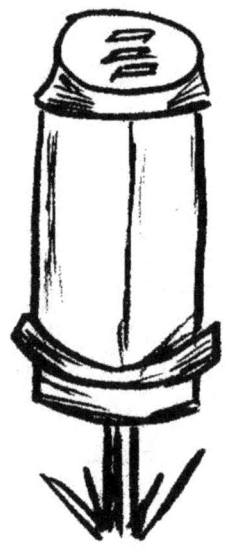

Illustration No. 7 The Yard Light

we glow brighter when display our powerlessness
chapter six

In 1993, my dad was diagnosed with a very rare cancer. From diagnosis to death, victims of this cancer are expected to live nine months at the most. Dad had already had his bouts with cancers. Just six years earlier, he had a melon-sized tumor removed from his abdomen. When they took out that tumor, they found a benign tumor on some arteries. And over the next few years, he had a half dozen other surgeries, removing benign tumors from his arteries and kidneys. Tumors also caused hernias in his torso. But in 1993, things changed.

There was no real way to treat the tumors caused by pheochromocytoma. Most people never know they have this type of cancer; their families hear about it after an autopsy is done. Dad fought the disease for six years, with tumors appearing on his adrenal glands, his gall bladder, and, ultimately, taking over his bone structure. Dad spent those years attempting to remove the tumors, undergoing nearly 300 sessions of radiation, and ongoing attempts to manage the pain. During that time, he heard from many people "what God had apparently told them to tell him."

Herbal remedies, exercise regimes, prayer conferences, and prophetic words were spoken to and over my dad. Now, my family and I all believe that herbal remedies, exercise regimes, prayer, and prophetic words have their place. They are all legitimate, powerful ways that people's lives are changed. But during these years, I can't count the times our family heard the words "God wants you to know ____," or "The Lord told me that ____," or "I saw in a vision that if you just__, you'd be healed." Dad was even told once that God had told someone that he'd "see his children's children's children." But my dad died on Good Friday of 1999. No one had the power to take away the cancer that was eating up my dad. No one had the strength to destroy these tumors. And no one had the power to move heaven or hell to cure this disease. He wasn't healed, he didn't see great-great-grandkids, and herbal remedies just left him hungry and with bad breath. Someone was wrong. And I don't think it was God.

"Healing" has been defined as "a completeness brought to a brokenness." Do you believe God can heal? Why do you believe that?

What role do you think humans take in the healing process?

One last way we glow is by the display of our powerlessness. Weakness is not sought after very much. We go to gyms and eat "power bars" and flex what we think is muscle, both physically and mentally. That little kid's song was so right: "I am weak, but He is strong." I really don't have that much power. I am ignorant of it. Now, I know that the Holy Spirit is dwelling in me, and that Jesus said it is in me, so I can do things even greater than He did. But when push comes to shove, many times, when I try to flex spiritual muscle, I am more likely to fall on my face than to display God's power. Elisha I am not.

This isn't a fair reflection of God's power. His power is awesome and constant and transforming. It's in me, but I wonder if that's what God wanted to show all the time. What little power I do have isn't changing the world. I met a lady who saw an obituary in the newspaper and went to the funeral home for the sole purpose of raising the person from the dead. She didn't know the person or their family, but she crashed the funeral and went up to the casket and started to pray that the person "arise and come forth" and all that. Again, God is capable of doing this, but there was no resurrection. You probably would have read about it.

I can't help but wonder what the family must have felt like after this display. Power was called down. None came. It was already a tough time for them, but then some stranger comes in and tries to fix things and only makes them worse. This lady "just knew this is what was supposed to happen." Apparently she didn't know after all. More followers of Jesus need to be using the words "I don't know" when they are talking with others. When I admit that I don't know the why's, how's and when's of life (rather than just fumbling my way through the tough answers to a tough life and complicating the situations that others are facing) I think it makes Jesus glow in me more. But this is obviously a hard thing for me, and for us, to admit.

Why do we think we need to provide answers or explanations for the things people are dealing with?

solar powered help

Why do I think I need to have all the answers to people's questions? Anytime someone around me is facing a difficult situation, just like that lady at the funeral home or all those friends of my family, I find myself saying the most unhelpful things. "Well, don't forget Jesus loves you." "God will work it all out." "God's ways are not our ways." "I can't wait to see what good God will bring out of this mess." It's not that all these things are false… it's just that sometimes the truth of these things we say gets in the way of living, hurting and healing.

We think pain is bad, so we try to remove it. We want to try to answer questions that we think people may have, and when we do answer, we spout some nice sentiments that do nothing to alleviate the pain of others. Most of them are pat answers, too. They gloss over the pain, confusion and frustration, and probably make things worse! We judge people just for experiencing natural responses to tragedies of all sorts. We try to explain the mind and ways of God and end up just talking nonsense, not listening, and hurting with those we love.

Those solar-powered lawn lights really don't make much of a difference in the illumination of a home. Spotlights are used for that. But these lights shine by just being there. They don't light paths too much. They don't make the house brighter or highlight the paint job. I doubt if many thieves are seriously deterred by the placement of ornamental lawn lighting. But these lights do offer some solace, comfort, and peace to the homeowner. It's just nice and reassuring to have them. Our light doesn't always need to be tangible. There is not always a tangible purpose to our glow. At times it needs to be the searchlight that exposes that which is misplaced, or the floor lamp that illuminates the truth which is there before us. But sometimes our light just needs to shine in dark situations, without our words or anything. Just by being there, we can glow.

Does our glow have to accomplish something tangible? Does the effect of our glow have to be seen in order for our glow to be valid?

A story is told about a little boy whose elderly neighbor had just lost his wife. Seeing the old man's pain, the little boy climbed the fence, hopped into the man's yard, jumped into the old man's lap, and just sat there. When his mom asked what the boy had been saying to the man, the child responded, "Nothing, mom. I was just helping him cry." Maybe sometimes we'd glow more if we talked less. If we didn't always try to give answers and excuses to eliminate the tears, and instead, helped people cry them.

shut your mouth

Job knew loss. Everything he had was ripped from him in some cosmic bet that he'd still follow God.

(This still doesn't make sense to me that God would do this; but who am I to tell God He was out of line!?) His kids, wife, wealth, and health were all robbed and destroyed. It was obvious to all around that he was not in good shape. His friends noticed and did the most helpful thing. At first. Job's friends did the most good when they just sat there and didn't say anything.

> When three of Job's friends heard of the tragedy he had suffered, they got together and traveled from their homes to comfort and console him. Their names were Eliphaz the Temanite, Bildad the Shuhite, and Zophar the Naamathite. When they saw Job from a distance, they scarcely recognized him. Wailing loudly, they tore their robes and threw dust into the air over their heads to show their grief. Then they sat on the ground with him for seven days and nights. No one said a word to Job, for they saw that his suffering was too great for words.
> - Job 2:11-13 (NLT)

The rest of the book of Job is full of good "bad" examples from Job's friends. "Here's what I think about your problem, Job. "Have you tried this …?" "Maybe you'd be in a better place if you had only …" It was when they attempted to explain and instruct that they failed to represent God. Most of what they said to Job is so contrary to the Gospel.

We need to learn from Job's friends' examples and just shut up sometimes. To let people hurt, but also let them know we care. The words, "Can I pray for you?" will do so much more glowing than saying, "I think God is trying to teach you something here." I'm surprised how quickly a conversation turns when prayer support is offered. You may not even need to pray for them right then and there, unless the opportunity and desire for it is obvious. Thoughtful and prayerful concern goes a long way.

Have you ever experienced not knowing what to say, then saying the absolutely wrong thing? Or has something like that ever been said to you? How did you feel afterward?

Mike was a kid who lived across the street from me when I was growing up. He's the only person I've ever been in a fight with, twice. The first time, when I was in fourth grade, he said something mean about my third-grade girlfriend. I don't even remember what it was; only that I kicked his butt in my front yard.

About 20 minutes later, without prodding from my parents, I called his mom to apologize. The other time, when I was in high school, he stepped on my brother's face. So I beat Mike's face bloody. Again, about 20 minutes later, without prodding from my parents, I called his mom to apologize. Tough guy I am not.

One day when I was in college, my mom called and said Mike had killed himself. He decided he couldn't take it anymore and hung himself in his garage. Mike's mom found him, and my dad cut him down and tried to revive him, to no avail. Even though we beat each other up a couple times, the history Mike and I shared was full of more fun times than violent ones. I was devastated. I wasn't expecting this. Whenever we fought, I never wanted him dead. Oh! His folks must be hurting so bad right now! I was away at school with academic demands there that prohibited me from coming home. I didn't feel it was a good time to call Mike's folks. I wouldn't have known what to say if I'd been able to go to the funeral, not to mention the awkwardness of the situation over the phone.

So, I bought his mom and dad a card. It's still one of my favorite cards ever. I can never find it, so I buy blank ones and just write what it said inside: "Sometimes when you don't know what to say, it's just important that others know that you care. I care." Mrs. Belcher told me that was the most encouraging card she had received. It's definitely one of the most profound and encouraging ones I've ever given. I wish I'd written it. All I can do is attempt to apply it.

being there isn't just taking up space

I don't think all the people who spoke hopeful words to my dad and my family was trying to be mean or uncaring. I think they had great intentions. They really wanted to see my dad healed. So in a common and weird spiritual practice, they attached their warm wishes regarding the outcome of my dad's bout with cancer to the goodness found in The Almighty. But good intentions don't always take away people's pain. Often, we don't need to hear an assessment of the situation from people; we just need them to show and let us know they care.

This is all that Jesus asked of the disciples one night in the Garden of Gethsemane, the original olive garden. Just care. It's quite possibly the hardest time of His life, and Jesus wants nothing but companionship.

He didn't tell them, "Hey guys, can we kind of talk through some of the issues I'm facing?" He didn't say, "I need you guys to clear up some foggy areas of my life and explain the reasoning behind some of my feelings." "Just wait with me here," He said, an easy thing for the disciples to do. They'd accompanied Him on numerous occasions like this, I'm sure. "Jesus is gonna pray, and we're going with Him."

> Then Jesus went with them to the olive grove called Gethsemane, and he said, "Sit here while I go over there to pray." He took Peter and Zebedee's two sons, James and John, and he became anguished and distressed. He told them, "My soul is crushed with grief to the point of death. Stay here and keep watch with me."
>
> He went on a little farther and bowed with his face to the ground, praying, "My Father! If it is possible, let this cup of suffering be taken away from me. Yet I want your will to be done, not mine."
>
> Then he returned to the disciples and found them asleep. He said to Peter, "Couldn't you watch with me even one hour? Keep watch and pray, so that you will not give in to temptation. For the spirit is willing, but the body is weak!"
>
> Then Jesus left them a second time and prayed, "My Father! If this cup cannot be taken away unless I drink it, your will be done." When he returned to them again, he found them sleeping, for they couldn't keep their eyes open.
>
> So he went to pray a third time, saying the same things again. Then he came to the disciples and said, "Go ahead and sleep. Have your

> rest. But look—the time has come. The Son of
> Man is betrayed into the hands of sinners.
> -Matthew 26:36-45 (NLT)

Too bad they screwed it up. They couldn't even wait with Him. Sure, they didn't try to explain the problems away like Job's friends did. There was no "Jesus, I think you are facing your final hour because ..." No "You wouldn't be facing so much stress if You'd only ..." I'm glad the disciples weren't that stupid. But the other thing they didn't do was give Jesus the support He so desperately needed in those moments of turmoil.

What does it mean to "be there" for someone? Is that different than telling someone "I've got your back?" How?

Sure, the disciples were there physically. They showed up with Jesus, but didn't show up for Him. I really don't know how one supports God. God was clear that humans cannot offer any counsel to Him, so this

we glow brighter when we display our powerlessness

is obviously not what Jesus was looking for. I doubt He was in need of some comedic relief to divert His attention from the hour at hand. So what did Jesus need? Why did He ask them to come?

the lingering gift of empathy

Jesus went there to pray, so I'll assume that He expected this from the disciples. My dad always accepted the prayer of concerned friends and family. Thousands of people prayed for and over him during the years he was battling cancer. And my family still prays for sick people. The Bible tells us to do this many times. And people obeyed that scripture many times. Dad always felt that "maybe this time the prayer will move heaven, and I'll be healed."

So Jesus went off a little further into the garden to be alone, but that was no indication to the disciples that they were to take this as an opportunity for a nap. It is possible to pray for someone without knowing all the details. I know a person who wants all the specifics of the situations they pray for. They say this is so they know exactly how to pray for someone. I think too much information can get in the way of how I pray for someone. The thing I find myself lacking so much is a reliance on the Holy Spirit to direct my prayers for me. When I do this, I must wait. I must find silence in my prayer to hear the Spirit of God speak to my heart, so that I may direct my prayers about a situation back to Him. When my prayers are directed by what I know, I breeze through them. When they are directed by what I don't know, they are times of groaning, seeking, and empathizing with the ones I am praying for. Maybe this is something that Jesus wanted.

Can you see any other benefits to praying without knowing all the details?

Surely Job's friends would have benefited from relying of the Spirit of God to direct their words more than the things they thought they knew. A friend of mine is going through a divorce. It sucks that he has to deal with that stuff. He is such an awesome guy who loves Jesus and hunts for more and more ways to serve Him. He sought prayer at a church for this area of his life, and the dude praying for him just started jumping to some conclusions that were far from founded. The things he was praying over my friend were not even applicable! Then there was the accusation, condemnation, and a general glossing over of the magnitude of the situation. By the time "amen" happened, my friend was ready to punch the dude praying for him! One guy who prayed for my dad began apologizing to the Lord for my dad's lack of faith to be healed. What? Are you serious?! In both of these situations, had the people praying sought the Spirit's direction or taken the time to connect with the heart of God, perhaps something spiritual could have happened. But these were just words, connected to human thoughts, not divine intentions.

Empathy is a very different thing than sympathy. Sympathy makes us feel sorry for people. It's recognizing brokenness. It's easy for us to recognize, understand, and support the emotional and situational condition of someone and respond with compassion and sensitivity. The disciples were sympathetic to Jesus. It was obvious to them that Jesus was going through some turmoil. But empathy takes this a step further. With empathy, we co-experience the thoughts and emotions of another person. We hurt for them without attempting to express to them how they must be feeling. Sympathy can be felt for about anyone, but empathy is reserved for those who are close to us. Relationship is involved in empathy. And the benefit of this gift lasts so much longer than an "I'm so sorry you have to deal with this."

console versus counsel

Another thing Jesus may have desired from the disciples, beyond empathy, is consolation. Consolation is so different from counsel. Counsel says, "Let me help you fix this problem." Consoling is saying, "Let me hurt with you. Let me take some of your pain. Let me make sure you are okay while you hurt like this." Nothing the disciples said could have made facing the Cross any easier for Jesus. Jesus was crying and under so much stress that He was sweating blood! Where's the disciple asking what they can do to help Him? Where's the follower of Jesus pulling out a hanky to help Him clean up? Where's the drink of water Jesus surely could have used? Like in Job, where's the realization that "His suffering was too great for words?"

I'd like to think I would have cried with Jesus. That I'd have pulled up my own rock and knelt with Him, my arm around Him, and just agreed in prayer with Him. "Father, I don't want Him to have to drink this cup either! Please give Him the determination and the strength to do what You ask of Him. Show me what I can do to be a support to my Rabbi." I'd also like to think that I wouldn't have deserted Him like these guys did. But I'm sure I would have run for my life as well. And I would have slept right through my Savior's darkest hour.

What is the relationship between empathy and consolation?

I recall one person who did a smashing job with this during my dad's fight. My dad was the senior pastor of a Pentecostal church in the Midwest. And Perry was the associate pastor at this time. Perry would stop by the house and just hurt with dad. He couldn't take away the pain, but he sincerely asked God to. And Perry didn't try to explain away the condition dad was in, but he did help all of us see how great the Heavenly Father is in spite of the way our earthly father was hurting. There may have been others who did this, helping out with some of the mundane aspects of leading a church. I know people would bring meals by the house for my folks. And maybe Perry erred like Job's friends did on occasions. But I don't recall those times. All I remember is a great example of empathy.

the crying Christ

I remember that when dad died, I heard some of the dumbest statements of my life. My whole family was hurting. We felt like God had let us down. We were worried about what was next without dad around, in our home, and in our church. Here are a few examples: "Well, at least he's not hurting now." "God has a purpose in all of this." "I guess God wanted him in Heaven more than you wanted him here on earth." Are you kidding me? This is the best you can come up with to say? Not many people came up and just said, "Man, I don't understand it, but it really sucks."

One day when Jesus was out being a Messiah, He found out that His friend, Lazarus, had died. Some of the followers took off to go be with the mourners. I like what Thomas said about this in John 11:16: "Let us also go, that we may die with him." He could have been acting like a smart aleck. But this also sounds like empathy to me.

A couple of days later, Jesus went to the town of Bethany to be with Lazarus' sisters, His friends,

Mary and Martha. The funeral was over. Martha was weeping and understandably ticked off. "If you would have come when we told you Lazarus was sick, we wouldn't have had to bury Your friend! I've seen You heal people, so I know You could've healed Lazarus." Notice what Jesus does. He does speak a couple truths, but never attempts to explain away Mary and Martha's pain or the pain of those who were mourning with them. Instead, in one of the shortest, most profound statements about Jesus' ministry, The Bible says, "Jesus wept."

How does the picture of a crying Christ offer consolation to you during your times of grief and pain? Do you think your tears for others can have the same impact?

the power of powerlessness

If crying with the hurting was a way of life for Jesus while He was on earth, why has it been abandoned by His followers in lieu of explanations and commentary? I desire to be like my Jesus in as many areas as I possibly can. In the words "Jesus wept," I find a great way to glow: Shut up, empathize, console, and cry. What I think I know may hurt others. What I don't know may heal.

I truly wish I had the power to fix things, like it says in the Coldplay song, "Fix You." I think guys are worse at this than girls. We see tears, and want them stopped. We see something broken and we want to repair it. We see discomfort, and we want to make it comfortable. In my experience, when I have attempted to fix other people I have only made matters worse. No matter what strengths or gifting we may have, we cannot fix people. Even with the counseling I had while I went through my divorce, the trained counselor did not fix me. It wasn't him. But the opportunity to be heard, knowing that someone was experiencing my pain with me, and the chance to be connected with a crying Jesus, were just what the doctor ordered.

Henri Nouwen, in his book Gracias!, tells about being with a church in Central America. There was a lady at the church whose 18-year-old son, Walter, had died a week earlier. She wanted Henri to go to the cemetery with her, pray with her, and bless Walter's grave. When Henri met the woman, she was just sobbing. Walter was on one of those trucks like we see in the movies loaded down with produce, animals and people standing on the running boards. That's where Walter was standing ... until he lost his balance, fell under the wheels of the truck, and was crushed to death. And now his mom was crushed, too, and she wanted Mr. Nouwen's comfort. All the way to the cemetery, Walter's mom talked about what a great man Walter was; how he helped her so much in the home and served God at the parish. This is what Henri Nouwen did: "I couldn't keep my eyes off the woman's face, a gentle and deep face that had known so much suffering. She had given birth to eight children: seven girls and Walter. When I stood in front of the grave I had a feeling of powerlessness and a strong desire to call Walter back to life. 'Why can't I give Walter back to his mother?' I asked myself. Then I realized that my ministry lay more in powerlessness than in power; I could give her only my tears."

All the great people who die each week in the world, all the great prayers that are prayed for them and their families, and I've never read a headline that says "So-And-So Raised from the Dead!" I truly believe that God can do this. He's more than capable. And I truly believe He is capable of letting us demonstrate His heart by hurting with the people around us, not just trying to heal them. Perhaps, most of the time, God would rather we glow more in our powerlessness than in our power.

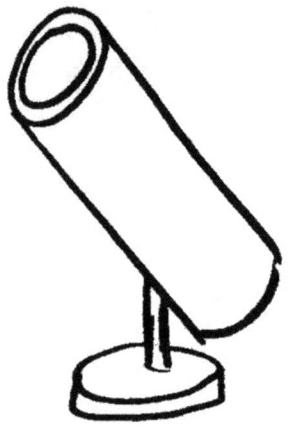

Illustration N°. 8 The Search Light

conclusion

There is no way that I have completely covered in the previous pages what it means to share your faith. Better books than this have been written explaining how to tell people about the difference Christ has made in people's lives. I do hope and pray you are looking at it differently after reading this book, though. Like when you see a banana. Maybe you'll ask yourself what is keeping you from telling people about the Jesus difference. When you see a disco ball, perhaps you'll ask yourself, "Is my glow starting a party? Am I infiltrating the darkness with the light of the world?" Or the next time you reach for a dimmer switch, maybe you'll take a look at what might be hindering God's light from shining through you. Or when you see a glow-in-the- dark Frisbee, you are reminded that time alone with God is invaluable. Or when you see a Glow Worm, hopefully you'll remember that the pressures you face can be used to let people see Jesus more clearly. Or when you see a glow-stick, you seek out humility and total dependence on God to sustain you.

Nonetheless, I'm certain that a number of people saw the word "conclusion" and thought, "What now? What do I do next?" Good questions. I think I have a simple answer: Do SOMEthing!

I have a friend who responds to many spiritual challenges with a four-word pat answer. If you ask her about joining a small group, supporting a mission work, or attending a conference, she'll respond with the words, "I'll pray about it." But she won't. That's her way of politely saying no. But it's pretty impolite. I wonder how many people are neutralized because they think praying about it is a more spiritual activity than getting into the thick of it and actually doing something.

Early on in this book, we identified and addressed some common reasons that we do nothing in terms of telling people about Jesus. I am convinced that God would much rather see you fail in His name than to sit on your "Blessed Assurance." Often I find myself waiting for a "move of God." Maybe God is waiting for a "move of Randy!" So seriously, what do you do next? Do something. Move. You can't just sit around hoping people will notice a difference in your life. However, I guess inactivity will result in people noticing a difference. They'll notice how fat you're getting. Hundreds of thousands of people who follow Jesus feed on sermons and lessons every weekend, and do nothing with it. For years they have eaten 52 meals a week and never exercised. So do something.

Do you think there's a problem with hearing sermons and lessons without exercising what is taken in? Why?

i have the power

Remember He-Man? I am a little too old to remember the details, but my brother grew up watching him. I remember one thing about that goofy cartoon. He-Man would hold up his sword and in a mighty voice he'd say "I have the power!" And lightning would come down and equip He-Man to do the unthinkable. Well, you and I have power from on high, and we don't need to look like cheesy cartoon super heroes to use it.

In Acts 1:8, Jesus said that we'd receive power from the Holy Spirit, and that we'll be His witnesses in Jerusalem, Judea, Samaria, and to the ends of the world. For now, let's just look at the first part: "And you will receive power when the Holy Spirit comes upon you …" I believe that the Holy Spirit is active in a lot of people's lives, not just those who swing from chandeliers and have big hair on those religious TV shows. When we come into a relationship with Jesus, His Spirit takes over our lives. As it says in Galatians 2:20: "I no longer live, but Christ lives in me." We have all the power we need to impact our world in huge ways! The Holy Spirit, the power source, is living in us. And I think it wants to glow out of us like we were in that movie Powder.

Read Acts 1:1-11. What role do you play in God's plan to tell the world what He's all about?

I have seen many failed methods of evangelism. Street witnessing, door to door evangelism, big tent revivals. I'm sure they all had their place at some time, and when society changed, the method of offering Jesus' gift of salvation needed to change too. When I was growing up, "friendship evangelism" was all the rage. To many, it boiled down to hoping and praying someone would notice you were a Christian, and then they'd ask you about it. Really? We're going to put Jesus' command to "go" into a new format that says "I hope you notice?" I am not a fan.

I sincerely hope you didn't get a friendship evangelism vibe from this book. I think that is a copout. And I would strongly encourage being driven by a bit more purpose than "I hope someone notices so I can talk to them about Jesus." Within the faith community, the image of a lighthouse has been popular for decades. Lighthouses have been painted, sculpted, and tattooed. Churches and stores have been named "lighthouse." I grew up in Iowa. I didn't see many real lighthouses. Even now, I live 10 minutes from the California coastline, and I still don't see lighthouses. I hear there's one around here, but I see more Lighthouse Churches than actual lighthouses. Now if you have lighthouses around you, feel free to picture those. I don't regularly see them. I understand what they do; I just want a point of reference I am more familiar with.

it's all about the missing

I do see a lot of searchlights. And I saw them a lot in the Midwest, too. They don't make good names for churches or stores though: First Searchlight Church or Sky-Tracker Books and Bibles? No. But I am going to suggest that a good picture of what to do next can be illustrated by searchlights, like the ones you've seen at airports. Not the ones on the runways that guide planes in (although there is some good application there, too). I'm talking about the ones that spin around in wide sweeping circles.

Just like a searchlight is all about the missing, I think the Holy Spirit gives us the power to be all about the missing in a couple ways.

the guiding Light

The first way we are empowered is to be guiding lights. If I am not near an airport and I see search lights shining in the sky, I wonder what's going on. Often, I will redirect my car and drive toward the lights to see what the big deal is. It's usually a grand opening of a restaurant or a store or something. But those searchlights make me change direction.

That's one purpose of searchlights. Lighthouses and airports have these searchlights on them so that ships and planes can get their bearings when the fog or storms knock them off course. Airports have runway lights that do this, too. God knows I've been knocked off course by the storms of life or by the fog that fills my head at times. All of us occasionally need this redirection.

You and I are agents of God, assigned to help people redirect themselves toward God. I graduated from a small Christian liberal arts school with a double major in Philosophy and Communications. This equipped me to work in the food service industry for about six years after college. Let me be the first to confess that I did not always do a good job of reflecting Jesus in my workplace. I failed often. But in spite of my weakness, people would truly seek me out for advice or guidance. One time, a manager approached me and said, "Randy, do you think I'm going to hell cuz I am sleeping with my boyfriend?" I had an opportunity to tell her about a God who hurts because of our sin. A God who hurts when we do as our sin eats us apart, yet, one who gave a solution to that problem. A customer and I had a great, candid discussion one day about whether or not he was born gay. Another customer asked "Why do you treat the homeless guy and that CEO exactly the same way?"

In these situations and countless others, people initiated conversations with me about life, but the Holy Spirit in me began to shine like a searchlight, and I was used to bring people into a natural conversation about Jesus. Early on in this book, I said that people respond to light either like roaches or flies. Pay attention to those flies. They are drawn to the light.

This is a step past the whole friendship evangelism thing. I wasn't waiting for people to ask me a spiritual question. Rather, I was looking for opportunities to talk about Jesus without it seeming forced or cheesy. The Holy Spirit is active in people's lives even before they decide to accept His gift of salvation. We can call them "seekers" or "pre-Christians" or even "the lost." Paul called them "outsiders." I think they are the ones Jesus misses the most. He gave His life so they could be directed to His arms. And my part of the grand story is often just following the nudge of the Holy Spirit and being a natural place for them to go for redirection and guidance.

How can you tell when the time is right to talk to someone about Jesus?

Again, my job is not to try to close the deal each time. I am responsible for being a witness, telling what I see. When the customer asked about whether I thought he was born gay, the conversation did not end in him asking me to introduce him to some girls. In fact, Andy died of AIDS a few years later. But opportunity arose for me to tell him that God didn't "hate fags", despite the signs that some Christians hold at gay-pride rallies. Rather, I told Andy that Jesus loved him even if he never decided to look at Jesus' face ever again. And I told Andy that he'd be hard pressed to find any other man who'd treat him better than Jesus would. It was a great talk, but Andy died a gay man with a terrible disease, and he never accepted Jesus' gift of salvation. But he made that choice, not me.

The customer who asked about why I treated people with decency and equality ended up a bit differently. We had a great talk about how Jesus served everyone the same. And I wasn't expecting a better tip from the homeless guy; I just wanted to be like Jesus in everyway. I explained that Jesus didn't die "more" for some people than others depending on their yearly income or professional status. The man was intrigued, and we began a series of regular discussions about my faith versus the way he saw faith growing up. Last I knew, he and his wife had started going to church again and he was a deacon at his church, serving in any way he could.

When have you had a conversation that led to a spiritual discussion like the ones described in this book?

the search of searchlight

One way we are like guiding lights is to shine as a place for the missing to get their bearings and redirect. The other way is to go out and search for the missing. I'm not sure if you noticed, but the word "search" is part of "searchlight." When I was a kid, my little brother went missing. He was about three years old, and we couldn't find him anywhere. We searched the house. We searched the church right next to our house where my dad was the pastor. We search the alley behind our house. We called our neighbors to help, and they searched all over. Nothing. We called the police, and they searched. They finally found my brother at a nearby drug store, eating M&Ms. He'd wandered off, walked a couple of blocks away, and was standing in a busy intersection when a Good Samaritan brought him to the drugstore and called the police. He was unharmed, but I think that incident knocked a few years off the lives of my parents.

If you've ever lost something valuable, like a little brother, you know how desperate the search is. Jesus compared the Kingdom of God to that search a few times. In Luke 15, Jesus tells three stories about things that go missing: a sheep, a coin, and a son. And in each situation, the search was on. Jesus said that each of these stories illustrates what God's Kingdom is like. The missing are valuable to Him.

Read Luke 15. Why do you think Jesus chose a lost sheep, a lost coin, and a lost son to tell about how important the missing are to Him?

In Jesus' parables, a shepherd leaves 99 sheep to find one lost one; a woman gets all her friends to help her look for a missing coin; a dad stands in the driveway looking for his son to return. The value of what was missing grows incrementally in these stories. A lost sheep was the shepherd's livelihood. A lost coin? It was part of this woman's dowry, her future. A lost son was all about legacy and influence, and a whole lot more personal than a sheep or a chance of finding a mate.

No matter how insignificant or how lofty the missing person or thing, Jesus is committed to the search. As His hands and feet, we should be just as committed. Paul encouraged the early church to "walk circumspectively." We don't use that word so much anymore, but it means to keep and eye out all around us, just like a searchlight looking for the missing during an emergency. Paul goes on to say that we are to "make the most of every opportunity." What opportunities did you have today, this week, or this month to tell others about how God has been a part of your story? Or how have you been a part of His?

In the chapters of this book, you have read about how to increase your glow. Now look for ways to glow into similar situations. When your coworker seems to be on a spiritual search, maybe spending time in the Son, come alongside her and glow. Illuminate a little more about her story by sharing yours. When your neighbor is stressed out and under pressure, that's an opportunity for you to introduce your story of how you weren't crushed when the pressure was on. When your sister- in-law is at the end of her rope, broken and humbled with no strength left, let her know about that time when you realized that Jesus was the only way you'd make it. Or, when your boss feels totally powerless, don't forget to cry with him.

an answer to Jesus' prayer

Asking God to help you recognize opportunities to tell people about Him is a prayer He will undoubtedly answer. The real challenge here is to notice where God is at work in a person's life, and then join Him in the work He is doing. Not to take over the work for Him. And if you are worried that you won't be able to tell where He is working, ask Him to show you. I've heard that "you can't talk to people about God until you first talk to God about people." I don't know if that is a theologically sound statement, but I do know that these are the kind of prayers God gets giddy about answering. Ask God to help you see the opportunities. "God, who should I pray for today, even if they are strangers?" "God, don't let me miss a chance to let people know what you are doing in my life." Remember; you have the power.

What's more, you have Jesus' prayer support. In John 17:20, Jesus prays and says, "I'm praying not only for them, but also for those who believe in me because of them and their witness about me." Jesus is asking God to help you be His witness. And He prays for the people you haven't told about Jesus.

Read John 17. What does it mean to you that Jesus prays for you this way?

How will you respond to His prayer?

It's kind of weird to think that Jesus is praying for me and for the people I encounter. It's scary and humbling that He trusts me with His message. I forget to buy everything on my grocery list at the store almost every week! This week, I forgot to buy coffee four days running. And yet God trusts me with His message. It's kind of overwhelming that He wants me to be a part of His plan to renew and restore people. Not to do the restoration, only He can do that, but to tell people about Him. And it's kind of overwhelming, in writing this book, I was asked to encourage you to actively participate in what He's doing in the world. It's also kind of humbling that you are still reading about it in my book.

no really, this is the conclusion

So, we've identified some dimmer switches and we've uncovered a handful of ways that increase our glow. The next logical question is, "Where do I start glowing?" It may mean glowing in ways and places that most wouldn't understand. You may be scrutinized and face objections from religious people around you. I know a girl who worked for a Christian daycare who was trying to glow Jesus to friends who didn't follow Him. She reflected Christ to them in some dark places. The Pharisees who ran the school didn't understand what she was doing, and took steps to assure her exit from their employment. Some who follow Jesus may never understand the way you glow.

They aren't always supposed to, though. They already have the light; or they should.

Like Jesus said, "It's the sick that need a doctor." It's the rotting or the bland that need the salt. It's the dark that needs the light.

Jesus recognized this so much that we sing about it in a popular worship song: "Light of the World, He stepped out into darkness." Man, I am so glad He did! Think about it. Where would any of us be had Jesus chosen to remain in His well-lit Heaven instead of stepping into our dark world? All darkness is is the absence of light. Where will your friends who live in darkness be if you don't step out into their darkness? Follow Jesus' lead and take a step into an area of the world that needs Jesus.

There are many people who want to change the world, but there are few who want to start where they are. I know a lot of people who think that in order to do any missions work, they have to go someplace else. Summers are full of church groups going to Mexico, Cuba, or Africa. I love this. I think it is so important. But I rarely hear of a summer mission's trip to the bad part of town or to an apartment complex across the street. Or a summer missions trip to an area shelter. In Acts 1:8, Jesus said that He wants us to tell people about Him everywhere—in Jerusalem, Judea, Samaria, and to the ends of the earth. I currently have no plans of going to any of those places! This is not a matter of geography; it is a matter of location. Glowing doesn't start at the uttermost parts of the earth. The best place to start glowing is where you are. The people Jesus said this to were already in Jerusalem. Where are you reading this? It's a great place to start glowing!

I'm at the airport as I write this, getting ready to go to Nashville on business. Some guy just came up to me and handed me a little flier. Apparently he is "the Professor of Hypnotism." It's an invitation and coupon for his hypnosis and mind control show at a nightclub in New Orleans. Everyone who has looked at this green piece of paper has read it, looked at him, read it again, and waited to talk to him. "Is hypnosis for real?" "What's the funniest thing you've ever seen someone do under hypnosis?" "How long have you been a hypnotist?" "Where'd you learn it?" I personally think it's kind of freaky, but this man has the attention of the terminal right now. Why can't a follower of Jesus like me be this dynamic and charismatic? (Not in a demonstrative and Charismatic way, but in a drawing people sort of way!) I think I know why. It's because I choose to turn off my glow.

Here I sit at the airport. Quiet. Not saying a word. Not sharing the mind altering effects of the presence of Christ. Not mentioning the time a preacher knew the innermost secrets of my heart through the Holy Spirit's revelation. I won't share how long I've been a follower of Jesus, or where I learned about Him. Or about that one time when the pastor mispronounced that one word that totally changed the meaning of the text. That was so funny. I won't even share how I know that a lot of faith seems hokey; yet, I know that it is real, and I can introduce them to a Person Who can help them be real in whatever amount of faith they have. I suck.

I can't change the world if I won't let the presence of Christ change my life. Is there something magical that makes you glow in another country when you can't glow in your own? The best place to start glowing is in your relationship with Jesus, spending time in the Son. Next, make sure that you are broken before Him. Your family will notice this. Your coworkers will, too. I'll bet that your small group will be transformed too, if just a few of us represented Jesus like this. It's a burning within that glows out of you. From there, I bet your neighbors will notice. They may even ask about it. When my wife and I found a for sale sign in the front yard of our rental last year, the neighbors hopefully saw a couple who believed God would provide a new place to live. When my daughter broke her collar bone, I trust that they saw a family who believed in the healing of the Great Physician. When I go through a divorce, the murder of my friends, the death of my dad, or whenever life's various pressures come on, those around me should be able to see that my faith in God sustains me. As these opportunities continue and I face painful times, I hope that these instances will be further times of reflecting Jesus.

Before long, it won't be just my family, coworkers, and neighbors who see Jesus at work. They'll start talking about what they've seen and encountered. "He's so not like the Christians I see on TV!" Next, the neighborhood has heard. Then a faith community or a church is impacted like never before. A new wind of renewal blows through! It revolutionizes the community and begins to impact the city. That city is rocked by the reality of individual relationships with Jesus Christ, and it spills over to the suburbs and towns. Soon the state is full of revival fire we only read about happening in the remotest regions of Brazil. As a few states encounter this, a nation is moved by the presence of God. Now we are ready to take it to the world.

And, yes, I do believe this is possible. Eleven Disciples of Christ glowed so brightly that you picked this book up or a friend of yours did, and gave it to you. The course of history was changed because a small group of people couldn't help but let others know about the difference Jesus made and was making in their lives. They glowed. What this book has said from the beginning isn't revolutionary or uniquely profound. I think others have probably said it in better ways than me. I just wanted to glow what God has illuminated in my life. It's natural. I can't help it. I just glow. Or at least I want to. But you picked up this book I wrote. So, kick the lights on. Start the music. Let the party begin. A disco ball is in waiting. Let's glow!

I kind of wish Jesus had said "Glow into all the world," instead of "Go."

Read 1 Peter 3:13-18. Is there a connection between our worship of Jesus and our empowering to tell people about Him?

This book started with a story about a guy who wanted God to give him the opportunity to talk about Jesus with someone during the next 24 hours. Join me in praying that you have that opportunity, too.

references

All scripture quotations are taken from the New Living Translation, copyright 1996. Used by permission of Tyndale House Publishers, Inc., Wheaton, IL 60189. All rights reserved. www.newlivingtranslation.com

Introduction

7-Eleven – To find a 7-Eleven near you, go to www.7-eleven.com. It's a lot easier than hijacking a car and driver.

Rick Warren – Rick Warren pastors the California mega-church, Saddleback. Find out more about Rick at www.rickwarren.com.

The Fear Factor – Fear Factor was a reality stunt/dare TV show that ran on NBC from 2001-2006. To see some daring and creepy stuff, check out www.nbc.com/Fear_Factor/.

Wendy's – The Wendy's Old Fashioned Hamburgers was founded by Dave Thomas in 1959 in Cincinatti, OH. For some really tasty fast food, find a Wendy's at www.wendys.com.

Biggie-Size – Biggie-Size was Wendy's extra-large servings of fries and drinks. They expired the Biggie-Size option in 2006, probably because Wendy's patrons were becoming Biggie-Size.

Saint Patrick – For a great look at how Saint Patrick reached out to the Celts, read George Hunter's book The Celtic Way of Evangelism, published by Abingdon Press in 2000.

U.S. Postal Service – Before there was a send button, there were stamps and envelopes that government employees hand delivered to your home. Support your government by using their service. Grandma wants to hear from you. www.usps.com

G.E. – General Electric was founded in New York in 1878. They specialize in electronic appliances, but they also own power companies, light, oil, gas, and NBC. www.ge.com

Chapter 1

Barry White – This music producer and singer/songwriter won five Grammy Awards in his lifetime (1944-2003). He is known for his deep, baritone voice that floated over some of the best R&B and soul music recorded in the 1970s.

Chic – Founded in 1976, Chic brought the cool factor to American funk and disco. "Le Freak" was their huge hit in '78. Since then, guitarist Niles Rogers has put his name on most of the great records of the last few decades.

KC & The Sunshine Band – Hailing from the Sunshine State in 1973, this funk/R&B/disco group penned songs that still make families laugh at that one uncle at weddings, including "Shake Your Booty," "That's the Way," and "I'm Your boogie Man." Find out if they are playing near you at www.heykcsb.com.

Bee Gees – The Brothers Gibb began making sappy soft rock ballads in the late 60s. then disco happened, and my sister bought an 8-track. To get your fix, check out www.beegees.com.

Saturday Night Fever – This 1977 film about disco dancing stars John Travolta and that girl who played his dance partner. The soundtrack is more popular than the movie.

Netflix – Before Netflix, people actually had to leave their house to watch movies. www.netflix.com

Funkytown – Lipps, Inc. recorded a pop masterpiece in 1980. It reached number 1 on Billboard's Hot 100 and Dance charts that same year. If you are looking for a place that keeps you movin', keeps you grooving; with some energy, Funkytown is your ticket to that place.

The Smashing Pumpkins – Smashing Pumpkins formed in Chicago in 1988. Led by Billy Corgan, the band was a hybrid of many rock styles and was responsible for some of the best music and videos from the 90s. www.smashingpumpkins.com

Pearl Jam – Rising from the rain puddles of Seattle in 1990, Pearl Jam co-led the whole grunge-rock genre. Their debut album, Ten, was criticized as being a corporate cash-out. But 20-some years later, the band is still touring hard and making fabulous music. www.pearljam.com

The Red Hot Chili Peppers – In 1983, Los Angeles got crazier and weirder when the funk-rock band the Red Hot Chili Peppers was formed. Their music has tamed over the years. www.redhotchilipeppers.com

Stevie Wonder – Stevie was born in 1950, and was signed to Motown eleven years later. His best songs are, well, all of his songs. He's still playing for fans around the world. www.steviewonder.net

"Higher Ground" – Okay, maybe this is the best Stevie Wonder song. It's found on all his greatest hits records, but originally appeared on Interventions in 1973. It hit #4 on the U.S. Pop Singles Charts, and #1 on the Hot Soul Singles.

E.T. – See it. It's a 1982 Stephen Spielberg masterpiece about a stranded alien and the little boy who befriends him.

Drew Barrymore – Born in 1975, Drew found breakout success starring in E.T. After some chemical abuse struggles, Drew turned herself around is a sought after actress today. www.drewbarrymore.com

Miracle Gro – Gardens across the U.S. are healthier and produce bigger vegetables as a result of this chemical mixture from the Scott's company. www.scotts.com

Steven Spielberg – Think of a classic film in the last 30 years. Spielberg probably had a hand in it. I'd tell you about the achievements of this filmmaker/screenwriter/producer/director/video-game designer, but that would be a book in and of itself. That's what happens when you have a 60-year career of successes.

Reeses Pieces – Yum. Candy-coated chocolate and peanut butter. The candy was introduced by Hershey's in 1978, but didn't catch on until the little pieces had a role in the film E.T. Now they are regularly in my wife's purse and our candy dish.

A.W. Tozer quote – I found this in the book The Best of A.W. Tozer, in an essay called "Why We Are Luke Warm About Christ's Return," published by Baker Book House Company in 1978.

"This Little Light of Mine" – Harry Dixon Loes wrote this song around 1920, and it's become a folk-favorite children's song.

Steve Taylor lyric – Quote taken from the song "Guilty By Association" found on the 1984 album Meltdown. If you can find any of his records, buy them. His satirical lyrics ring more true each year, although he hasn't made a record of his own since 1993.

Todd Agnew – This Christian singer/songwriter wrote a brilliant song called "My Jesus" for his 2005 album Reflection of Something. www.toddagnew.com

NAACP – The National Association for the Advancement of Colored People has been fighting for civil right for a century, but has yet to change their name. www.naacp.org

Chapter 2

The Purpose Driven Life – This devotional book by Rick Warren took the nation by storm in 2002, leading readers on a 40-day spiritual journey. The book from Zondervan Publishing has sold over 30 million copies. You'd think 30 million purpose driven people would be making a bigger impact...

Facebook – In February of 2004, social networking changed forever. As of this writing, more than 500 million people are connecting with people all around the world. www.facebook.com

Twitter – Two years later, another social networking option appeared. Tweets allow users to "microblog" about their happenings. www.twitter.com

McDonald's – The Golden-Arches first opened in 1940, and are now the world's largest fast-food chain. McDonald's serves more than 58 million customers each day. I have rarely walked out of their doors saying the words, "I'm Lovin' It." www.mcdonalds.com

Arby's –Known for their roast beef sandwiches and curly-fries, Arby's is a little step up the fast-food ladder from McDonald's. They are owned by the same company that owns the Wendy's chain of restaurants. www.arbys.com

"Every Move I Make" – David Ruis wrote this worship song that has been sung in thousandands of churches every Sunday since it was written in 1996.

The Gap – Since 1969, The Gap has been outfitting adults, kids, and babies. www.gap.com

Seinfeld – Seinfeld was an NBC sitcom that ran from 1989 through 1998. The show's nine seasons were based on the stand-up comedy of Jerry Seinfeld. Syndicated reruns will be on a cable station in just a few minutes.

Light the Night – This is the annual nationwide fundraising walk to benefit The Leukemia and Lymphoma Society. Join the walk this year! www.lightthenight.org

PTA – Parent Teacher Associations are at almost every school in the U.S. The parent led group helps raise money for educational purposes. www.pta.org

Big Brothers - Big Sisters – Big Brothers Big Sisters is a youth mentoring organization, connecting kids with healthy relationships with adults that positively impact their development. www.bbbs.org

World Vision – Since 1950, World Vision has been dedicated to organizing relief and development operations around the world. The easiest way to get involved is to sponsor a child. My family has been sponsoring a boy from Africa for years. Your family can sponsor a child, too, by visiting www.worldvision.org

The Mocha Club – By giving up just two mochas a month, members of the Mocha Club are impacting development efforts in Africa. Join the club here: www.mochaclub.org

Chapter 3

Mickey Mouse – Walt Disney created the cartoon character Mickey Mouse in 1928. Tourists in Anaheim, CA and Orlando, FL board airplanes wearing his ears every day. www.disney.go.com/mickey

Scooter – Scooter is the backstage "gopher" for The Muppets.

Muppets – The Muppets are a group of puppets created by Jim Henson. TV shows, movies, and TV commercials have been built around these hand-stuffed characters. www.muppet.wikia.com

Oompa Loompa – Oompa-Loompas are fictional characters hailing from Loompaland created for Ronald Dahl's books Charlie and The Chocolate Factory and Charlie and the Great Glass Elevator. In the 1971 film adaptation, they were orange skinned.

Frisbee – Although generally used to refer to all recreational flying discs, the Wham-O company actually owns the name.

For a wonderful elaboration of the rhinoceros reference here, check out the book The Barbarian Way by Erwin Rafael McManus, published in 2005 by Thomas Nelson Publishers. While you are at it, check out all of his books; he's a great writer.

Oswald Chambers quote – Paraphrased from the March 22nd entry in Oswald Chambers' devotional classic, My Utmost for his Highest. www.utmost.org

Home Depot- Even a home projects failure like me can get the help needed from the helpful staff at Home Depot. This chain of big box stores is packed full of home improvement and construction tools and supplies. You have no excuse for that squeaky board or leaky faucet. www.homedepot.com

Chapter 4

Glo-Worm – The Glo-Worm was created by Hasbro's Playskool division in 1982. When you squeeze it, its face lights up. Some Glo-Worms play a lullaby. The stuffed toy has gone through many metamorphoses, and there is one in my baby's room right now.

Tim Hughes- Tim is a worship leader from London. I'm certain you've sung one of his songs without even knowing it. www.timhughesmusic.com

"He's Got the Whole World In His Hands" – This song is found on Tim's second CD, When Silence Falls. Again, do not confuse it with the children's song with the same name.

Chapter 5

Ralph Torres – Ralph pastors the Pasadena Foursquare Church.

Glo-Stick – I use the term Glo-Stick to refer to any translucent tube filled with liquids that illuminate when broken.

Jack Hayford – Pastor Jack was born in 1934 and pastored The Church on the Way in Van Nuys, CA. He was president of The International Church of the Foursquare Gospel, Chancellor of King's University, and has written nearly 50 books. There is plenty to learn from this man. www.jackhayford.org

Flock of Seagulls – This 80s band is known for their well moussed coifs and for their contribution to the new-wave musical cannon. Their biggest song was "I Ran (So Far Away)," but I'm a fan of "Space Age Love Song." They are still playing shows. www.myspace.com/aflockofseagulls

Calvin Klein Obsession – This fragrance was all the rage in the late 80s when it launched for both men and women. Smell for yourself at your favorite department store.

Chapter 6

Olive Garden – The Olive Garden is a chain of restaurants that specializes in Italian-American food. I swear this is the last restaurant reference in this book… www.olivegarden.com

Coldplay – Formed in 1987, this English rock band took the world by storm with their first single "Yellow." Every song on every album is a masterpiece. (But they are not my favorite band…) www.coldplay.com

Henru Nouwen – Gracias - Henri Nouwen was a Dutch priest who penned over 40 books about spiritual growth. Gracias is Nouwen's journal from time spent ministering in Latin America, and was published by Orbis Books in 1993.

Conclusion

He-Man – He Man was created by DC Comics. He spent his time defending Castle Grayskull from Skeletor. Homes across the nation had the same mock battles lived out in their living rooms by imaginative little kids.

Masters of the Universe – The animated series began in 1983. The live action film released 4 years later. If you are still interested, check out www.he-man.org.

Sky Tracker – Sky-Tracker Searchlights are leaders in powerful promotional advertising searchlight rentals in the Southeast. I saw them used on a trip to Atlanta while writing this book. www.skytrackeronline.com

M&Ms – These candy-coated chocolates are known to "melt in your mouth, not in your hands." The candies have changed since they were created in 1941, and most of their varieties will be available in my home at some time or another this year.

acknowledgments

This book is the result of a lot of people around the country speaking into my life.

First of all, to my wife, Sally. Thank you for being the kind of woman who supports her husband and encourages him to do things that he thinks he is incapable of. I'm afraid of the day you'll really see that I am not as great as you see me, but I am so thankful for your cloudy vision. I love you, sweetheart.

Audrey, you are the best. If I could choose to do only one thing with my life, it would to be your dad. It would take more words than are in this book to tell you how much I love you.

Thanks to Lily. You are an angel who is yet to be born, but I already love you and would do anything to make your life great. See ya soon!

Mom, you and dad are the best parents I could ask for. You raised your kids to follow Jesus, and gave us great examples of what that means. I am proud to be your son, and only hope I can live up to the legacy that you and dad have established. And Ron, thanks for taking care of my mom. It does my heart good to see her love again.

Shelley, I so love you, sis. I miss shopping with you and going to see Def Leppard. You have always been the stabilizer in our family, making sure everyone is thought of, and not thinking of yourself nearly enough. You and Dan have raised three incredible girls whom I'd do anything for.

Perry, you are still my little brother. And I am proud of the man you have become. Honestly, who would have guessed it?! You and Carrie are a great couple and a wonderful story of Jesus making all things new again. I wish we could watch our kids grow up together.

Grandma Ella, your resilience to the challenges of life is a lesson to us all. I miss our trips to Gong Fu Tea and all over the state. I love you.

To Lion Mendoza and the historic Great Lakes District of Foursquare churches. This book came out of that first young adult's camp you invited me to speak at. That weekend at Camp Hickory is still one of my favorite ministry experiences ever.

To my home church at Evangel Chapel, thanks for letting me learn to teach. You trusted me with your kids, your spouses, and your parents. I pray that you ignored my youthful ignorance and only embraced the things that draw you closer to Jesus. To Pastor Robert and my current traditional church family at New Hope, thanks for letting me shave off the final rough edges of GLOW. Your excitement and support have been a capstone on this book. And to my simple church family, thanks for the safe place to peel back new areas of authentic expressions of what it means to follow Jesus.

To my Wellspring and Parable families, thanks for all the years of support and comfort and love. Bev, you have helped me enter areas of ministry and been a catalyst for where I am now. Steve, you are a true leader: you are going somewhere, and people follow you because you are one of the Godliest men I have ever met.

Rob, John, and John, you three pastors are some of my favorites. Not because you have the largest or coolest churches, but because you are the guys who supported me through my toughest times. You are truly some of my favorite people I have been privileged to call my friends.

Marilyn, I wouldn't have started working on this again without your encouragement. Your interest in what happened to this book years ago led to me finishing it. You doing okay?

Jeannie, Austyn, and Cindi, thanks for all your hard work making my words not look and sound goofy. Your excitement and constructive hands have made this book readable.

To Rob, Tammy, Tom, Chris, Todd, Michael, and Mary for letting me tell me tell about scenes from your stories. Surprise! To the churches, camp directors, and retreat leaders who were willing to let me share these messages with you. I think each of you has heard a different version of this! And if I forgot to thank you, it wasn't intentional. This is just going on and on and on… So write your name here: _____

And finally, and most importantly, thank you Jesus. May you receive the glory from this book, but most importantly may you glow exponentially through every person who reads this book.

randy ross
biography

Randy Ross has over twenty years of ministry experience to teens, college students, and young adults, ministering in over 400 churches from the Midwest to the West Coast. He holds a B.A. in Communications and Philosophy from Northwestern College. When he is not writing or listening to music, Randy works in marketing for The Parable Group, and lives on the Central Coast of California with his wife and two daughters. Wait, he writes and listens to music while he does all of that...

You can read Randy's blog at www.randy-ross.com.

Check out www.randy-ross.com/downloads for free resources!
Download the song "Glow" by DJ Magellan
Download GLOW group discussion questions for your book club.
Download the GLOW teacher's guide
Download GLOW hand-outs for your small group